D0990505

Natchez before 1830

The L. O. Crosby, Jr. Memorial Lectures
in Mississippi Culture, II

Natchez

before 1830

Edited by
Noel Polk

University Press of Mississippi
Jackson and London

1989

Copyright © 1989 by the University Press of Mississippi
All rights reserved
Manufactured in the United States of America
92 91 90 89   4 3 2 1

The paper in this book meets the guidelines for permanence and durability of the Committee on Production Guidelines for Book Longevity of the Council on Library Resources.

This book has been sponsored by the University of Southern Mississippi. The L. O. Crosby, Jr., Memorial Lectures in Mississippi Culture, 1987

Library of Congress Cataloging-in-Publication data

Natchez before 1830.

(The L. O. Crosby, Jr., memorial lectures in Mississippi culture ; 1987)
"Papers gathered here were delivered in Natchez, Mississippi, January 15–17, 1987, at the second of the L. O. Crosby, Jr., Memorial lectures in Mississippi Culture"—Introd.
Includes index.
1. Natchez (Miss.)—History—Congresses. I. Polk, Noel. II. Series.
F349.N2N28   1989   976.2′26   88-28046
ISBN 0-87805-380-8 (alk. paper)

British Library Cataloguing in Publication data is available.

Contents

Contents

Acknowledgments

The L. O. Crosby, Jr., Memorial Lectures in Mississippi Culture were established at the University of Southern Mississippi through a generous gift from the L. O. Crosby, Jr., Memorial Foundation, and through the cooperation and interest of Stewart and Lynn Crosby Gammill, whose wise counsel was an important part of every stage of planning the Crosby Lectures, from inception to fruition. Likewise, without the enthusiastic support of Dr. Aubrey K. Lucas, president of the University of Southern Mississippi, who made the resources of the university available to the organizers, the Crosby Lectures would not have come to be. To these three in particular the Crosby Lectures owe their existence, and I am grateful indeed for their support.

The Mississippi Committee for the Humanities also generously provided partial funding for the conference. To that organization and its director, Dr. Cora Norman, I extend heartfelt thanks; I am also grateful to Dr. Alfred Lemmon of the Historic New Orleans Collection for many favors. In Natchez, Margaret Moss and Ron Miller and the Historic Natchez Foundation, Ruth Ellen Calhoun, Ethel Green Banta, and Sarah Tillman, all played important roles in planning and executing the conference. Martha Furlong helped with many details and with proofreading. Finally, I am grateful to the USM Committee for the Crosby Lectures: Dr. Peggy W. Prenshaw, Dr. Thomas J. Richardson, and Dr. John D. W. Guice. I am grateful to them not just for their ideas, which helped identify topics, select speakers, and give shape and focus to the conference (indeed, made the idea of the Crosby Lectures a reality), but also for the many hours they spent working on the nuts and bolts of such a conference.

Introduction

The papers gathered here are those delivered in Natchez, Mississippi, January 15–17, 1987, at the second of the L. O. Crosby, Jr., Memorial Lectures in Mississippi Culture, a series established through the L. O. Crosby, Jr., Memorial Foundation with the express purpose of bringing together the best scholars available from a variety of academic disciplines to attend to areas of Mississippi history and culture that have been relatively unexplored.

At first, "unexplored" hardly seemed an appropriate adjective for Natchez; few cities in America can boast so colorful a history and it has in fact been looked at and looked at, and looked at again, and dreamed about and written about, by historian and novelist and romanticist, for years. There are ways in which this beautiful city is among the best-known of American towns. Sitting high atop the Mississippi River bluffs, it has in its long life been Indian village, European colony, frontier garrison, rough-and-tumble stopover for riverboatmen and gamblers, elegant and sophisticated home of wealthy planters, politicians, statesmen, carpetbaggers and scalawags, turbulent trading and economic center, and gathering spot for sportsmen and intellectuals. Because of its strategic location it became, in the early years of this country's development, the cultural and economic matrix for the great American Southwest: it was, as *The Mississippi Guide* put it, "an opulent, suave, and aristocratic community, maintaining a social and political prestige that influenced the entire Mississippi Valley." The history of this city and of this entire area is so rich, so intimately connected to American and European history, that it may truly be called fabulous, the stuff of which fables and legends are made. But in spite of its strong hold on the

American imagination—indeed, perhaps *because* of it—there are nevertheless many areas of Natchez history which have in fact remained
"relatively unexplored."

The conference we planned would try to divest Natchez of the many
myths that surround its history, to recover all that we could of the reality
of the daily lives of the people who had made the history. Thus a decision
was made not to deal with the Natchez Trace, a fabulous topic all by
itself, and not to deal with the immediately antebellum Natchez, a time
and place most rife with those myths which define "Natchez" almost
solely in terms of juleps and crinolines and hoop skirts, and to limit our
investigations to the historic period before 1830. In cooperation with the
Historic Natchez Foundation and the Historic New Orleans Collection,
this conference, "Natchez Before 1830," attempted to pry behind the
myths, to try to understand more about the various peoples who came
there and about the economic, political, and cultural forces which
shaped their lives in the lower Mississippi Valley.

In keeping with the interdisciplinary spirit of the Crosby lectures,
these papers represent the best efforts of scholars in a variety of disciplines to understand, from their own perspectives, the fascinating world
of Natchez before 1830. Ian Brown and Letha Wood Audhuy explore the
culture of the Natchez Indians, a complex civilization long before Europeans began exploring and settling the area. Brown, in "Natchez Indians
and the Remains of a Proud Past," draws on his own archaeological
expeditions to the Natchez sites and on the writings and sketches of
travellers such as Le Page du Pratz and Alexandre De Batz for his
portraits of Indian lifeways in the Natchez region. Audhuy, in "Natchez
in French History and Literature," demonstrates how Natchez has captured the imagination of the French people, largely through Chateaubriand's prose poem *The Natchez*, which centered on the Natchez
massacre of 1729. Indeed, in this work Chateaubriand made the episode
"assume epic, even mythical dimensions" as he "took up the myth of the
noble savage and brought it to its tragic culmination." Audhuy's discussion of the historical circumstances of the poem's composition—including the question whether Chateaubriand ever actually visited Natchez in
his travels—and her analysis of its literary qualities, are important
contributions to our understanding of Natchez's significance in Western
culture.

Alfred E. Lemmon's "Some Sources of Pre-1830 Natchez History in
Spanish Archives" and Don E. Carleton's "The Natchez Trace Collection" offer invaluable guides to virtually untapped archival material

essential to the study of the development of Natchez. The Spanish archives, Lemmon maintains, "contain a vast wealth of information for the reconstruction of Natchez under the Spanish 'Dons.'" Carleton's essay surveys the wealth of the Natchez Trace Collection acquired in December of 1985 by the Eugene C. Barker Texas History Center at the University of Texas. This collection, spanning the years between the late 1770s and the early 1900s, is a treasure trove, Carleton writes, "of original manuscripts, financial and legal records . . . maps, sheet music, newspapers, pamphlets, ephemera, photographs, diaries, and other archival documents of various description" whose contents "reflect the lives and activities of government officials, politicians, soldiers, bankers, farmer, jurists, planters, merchants, attorneys, physicians, clergy, educators, slaves, and homemakers who lived and worked in the parishes and counties of Louisiana and Mississippi, particularly in the region centered around Natchez." Milton B. Newton, Jr.'s, expert analysis, "Mapping the Foundations of the Old Natchez District: the Wilton Mapp of 1774," demonstrates precisely how Wilton's well-known map documents "the arrival of tangible British order upon the land of the Old Natchez District."

The last four papers in the collection attend to more quotidian aspects of life in Old Natchez. Morton Rothstein's "'The Remotest Corner': Natchez on the American Frontier" explores the beginnings of the Natchez economy. Rothstein describes the settlers' search for marketable products and their response to the various vicissitudes of political change and even revolution, by looking closely at the economic enterprises of three early settlers. His essay provides fascinating insights into the "human dimensions of [the] sweeping changes" in the late eighteenth and early nineteenth centuries. In "Well-Appointed: The Aesthetics of Everyday Life in Old Natchez," Estill Curtis Pennington proposes that "What we really want to know about a people is how they lived, and not only how they lived, but how the world in which they lived was appointed, or, if you will, furnished, and the flavor and color of their lives." Pennington does for the Natchezans of the late eighteenth and early nineteenth centuries what Ian Brown has done for the Indians of a century earlier. By examining the important surviving artifacts of their material culture—the silver, the furniture, and the portraiture—he tells us a great deal about how these people used their burgeoning financial resources to fill their daily lives with beauty, and so to bring the culture and refinement of the East to a rough and tumble frontier society. Jeanne Middleton Forsythe's "Education in Natchez before 1830" begins with the premise that "the practice of education reflects the society of which it is a part," since schools "pass on, from one generation to the next, the values, beliefs, and traditions that have defined that culture." She examines the "values, beliefs, and traditions" of Old Natchez as they are reflected in the various educational enterprises of pre-1830 Natchez. Her essay is an important summary of the education of men, women, and blacks (both free and, surprisingly, slave) during the period. Finally, Samuel Wilson's "The Architecture of Natchez before 1830" is a good deal more than a walking tour of some of the older Natchez buildings; it describes and places their architectural distinctiveness in the context of the history and of the place and the time, and provides much interesting and useful information about the architects and designers.

As with all of the Crosby Lectures, these papers are offered not as extensive answers to problems long discussed by historians, but rather as elaborate questions which have seldom been asked. Each contributor hopes that together, in their many interdisciplinary connections, these papers will suggest the numerous ways in which a wide variety of forces—cultural, historical, economic, political, even geographical—converged, sometimes with a vengeance, upon the peoples of the Natchez area, to shape and mold their daily lives, and that they will facilitate further discussion of the historic Natchez—the real one, rather than the mythical one of our collective imagination.

Natchez before 1830

Chronology of Natchez

JULIE SASS

1300–1600 a.d. Emerald Mound, second-largest Indian temple mound in the United States, is used by forerunners of the Natchez Indians.

1540 Natchez area is first explored by the Spanish under Hernando De Soto.

1541 De Soto discovers the Mississippi River.

1682 La Salle, representing France, and his followers stop in Natchez during their search for the mouth of the Mississippi.

1698 Iberville and Bienville establish the first settlement in Natchez.

1713 Antoine Crozat establishes a trading post among the Natchez. First black slaves are brought into Mississippi.

1716 French armed forces garrison Fort Rosalie, so named by Bienville after the Duchess of Pontchartrain.

1718 First plantation in Natchez is established by the Company of the West.

1721 Cotton is grown for the first time in Natchez.

1724 First indigo crop is harvested. The plant is abandoned many years later because of its damage to surrounding natural resources.

1729 Fort Rosalie massacre, November 28. Natchez Indians, tired of demands upon their territory, carry out a surprise attack upon the Europeans garrisoned there. Over 200 Europeans are killed; 300 women, children, and slaves are taken prisoner. Troops continue to be stationed at Fort Rosalie, but there is little or no settlement in the area for another 30–35 years.

1730   Yazoo Indians join the Natchez tribe in January for an uprising against Fort St. Peter. French Governor Perrier leads a reprisal against the Natchez. Most of the tribe is destroyed; others scatter into Choctaw and Chickasaw territory to the North, or are jailed in New Orleans and later sent as slaves to Santo Domingo.

1763   Treaty of Paris ends the French and Indian War. France cedes all territory east of the Mississippi River except the Isle of Orleans to Great Britain. Natchez is included in the Province of West Florida, whose government is based in Pensacola. Fort Rosalie is renamed "Panmure."

1765   Treaty between Great Britain and Choctaws gives Britain title to the District of Natchez.

1776   Governor Peter Chester continues liberal land grants, making Natchez a haven for loyalists.

1778   Settlements on the Mississippi River, including Natchez, are attacked by a force of 100 men, led by James Willing. Supplied with the authorization of the Continental Congress to secure supplies for the American army in New Orleans, Willing and his men loot and destroy Loyalist homes in the area.

1779   Spain declares war against Great Britain. The surrender of the British fort in Baton Rouge leads to a transfer of English settlements on the Mississippi River to the Spanish.

1781   A British revolt against Spanish rule in Natchez is defeated.

1782   Regulations are drawn for government in Natchez.

1783   Treaty of Paris: Great Britain cedes all territory east of the Mississippi River except the Isle of Orleans and north of 31 degrees to the United States. Spain is given control of the region south of 31 degrees, the British colony of West Florida.

1785   First census of the Natchez District shows 1619 people, including 498 slaves.

1789   Spanish invitations for American settlers in the Natchez area. The Spanish are generous with land grants. Manuel Gayoso serves as Governor until 1797.

1790   Treaty of Natchez, in May. A treaty of mutual respect between the Spanish and the Chickasaw and Choctaw nations. Simply, it states: "All the individuals of the Spanish, Chickasaw and Choctaw nations shall love one another reciprocally." The treaty provides justification for Spanish interference in Indian affairs.

1795   Pinckney Treaty between Spain and the United States cedes the Natchez area to America, and sets the 31st parallel of North Latitude as the recognized southern boundary of the United States.

1796   Eli Whitney introduces his cotton gin.

1797   In February Andrew Ellicott, the appointed Commissioner for the United States government, is sent to Natchez to claim the area from the Spanish. In March, a treaty with the Creek Indians gives the United States land for trading posts.

1798   On April 7 Natchez is made capital of the Mississippi Territory, under United States control. The boundaries are surveyed by Andrew Ellicott: longitude, 90.29.16 west of Greenwich; latitude, 31.33.48 north. In August Winthrop Sargent is named first governor of the Mississippi Territory. His cabinet includes John Steels (Secretary) and Peter Bryan Bruin, Daniel Tilton, and William McGuire (Territorial judges).

1799   First code of laws for the Mississippi Territory is created by Governor Sargent. Natchez District is divided into two counties, Adams and Pickering, named for the United States President and his Secretary of State.

1800   Postal route is established on the Natchez Trace, an old Indian trail. *Mississippi Gazette* published until 1802.

1801   United States gains permission to open the Natchez Trace across Indian lands: Treaty of Chickasaw Bluffs, with the Chickasaw Nation, in October; on November 23, the new Territorial Governor, W. C. C. Claiborne, arrives. Treaty of Fort Adams, with the Choctaw Nation, signed in December. Mississippi sends Narsworthy Hunter as its first delegate to the United States Congress.

1802   Capital of Mississippi Territory moved from Natchez to Washington. Jefferson College is established. Andrew Marschalk begins printing *The Mississippi Herald*.

1803   General Assembly of Mississippi Territory incorporates City of Natchez, with Samuel Brooks as mayor. Congress passes first comprehensive land law for the Territory, validating claims of those who had lands under cultivation before the Pinckney Treaty of 1795. Louisiana Purchase; area not opened to trade.

1805   Natchez Hospital is established. Supreme Court of the Territory established.

1806   United States Congress appropriates funds for a road along the

Natchez Trace, from Natchez to Nashville, Tennessee.

1807   Aaron Burr and his flotilla land in Bruinsburg, January 10. Burr trial in Washington, February.

1809   Bank of Mississippi is chartered as the first in the state; holds monopoly until 1830s.

1810   First serious effort to gain statehood is made.

1811   A bill is introduced in the Congress for the admission of Mississippi into the Union.

1812   In June, the United States declares war on Great Britain.

1813   Creek Wars fought by Creeks to prevent the spread of white settlements along the Tombigbee and Alabama Rivers in the eastern Mississippi Territory.

1814   Treaty between the United States and the Creek Nation gives America the right to establish military and trading posts, to navigate waters, to use and open roads in the eastern Mississippi Territory.

1815   The Natchez Rifles take part in the Battle of New Orleans. In December, British prisoners taken at New Orleans are brought to Natchez. The first river steamboat built in the interior of the United States, the *New Orleans*, arrives in Natchez from Pittsburgh.

1816   Elizabeth Academy is established.

1817   On March 1, President Madison signs an act dividing the Mississippi Territory and creating Alabama and authorizing a Constitutional Convention at Washington, Mississippi. In December, Mississippi is admitted as a state.

1820   Introduction of Mexican cotton into the state, a stronger and more easily-cultivated and -picked strain which, along with the cotton gin, helps make cotton into the predominant factor in the state's economy.

1821   In January, after much intense sectional rivalry, the General Assembly provides for the establishment of a permanent state capital near the geographic center of the state. Thomas Hinds, James Patton, and William Lattimore locate a suitable site; the new state capital is named Jackson, in honor of Andrew Jackson.

1822   Poindexter Code—a general revision and consolidation of the state's statutes—adopted by the General Assembly. In December, the General Assembly meets for the first time in Jackson.

1825   Marquis de Lafayette visits Natchez.

1827   Lt. Governor Gerald C. Brandon, of the Natchez District, becomes the first native Mississippian to be elected Governor.

1830   Planters' Bank is established in Natchez.

NOTE: This chronology is primarily based upon volume I of Richard Aubrey McLemore, ed., *A History of Mississippi* (Jackson: University & College Press of Mississippi, 1973), and especially those essays by Jack D. L. Holmes, "A Spanish Province," Robert V. Haynes, "The Formation of the Territory" and "The Road to Statehood," and Porter L. Fortune, Jr., "The Formative Period." Dunbar Rowland, *Encyclopedia of Mississippi History.* 2 vols. (Madison, Wis.: Selwyn A. Brant, 1907); ———. *History of Mississippi: The Heart of the South.* vol. 1. (Chicago: S.J. Clarke Publishing Company, 1925).

Natchez Indians and the Remains
of a Proud Past

IAN W. BROWN

Two-and-a-half centuries have passed since the Natchez rose up against
the French, yet there are still people in Oklahoma who have Natchez
blood flowing through their veins. The Spanish came, the English came,
and the French returned for a while, at least on paper. Flatboats laden
with corn and whiskey, and manned by rough-and-ready characters,
floated down the Mississippi headed for New Orleans. Midway between
that port and their homes on the Ohio River was Natchez, a haven to
those who had spent restless weeks on board makeshift vessels. As these
crafts approached the steep bluffs of Walnut Hills (now Vicksburg), there
must have been many a sigh of relief. Each man knew that Natchez was
near. As they continued down the river, by the mounds along its shore
they checked their progress. The mounds were built by the Natchez.[1]

The Natchez Indians were a small tribe compared to their eastern
neighbors, the Choctaw. Other southeastern groups such as the Cherokee, Creek, and Chickasaw also greatly outnumbered them, but the
Natchez were distinct; they alone had a complex chiefdom that was ruled
over by a Great Sun, an individual who had the power of life and death
over his subjects. Nowhere in the eastern woodlands was there such a
society in early historic times.[2] Ironically, the Natchez themselves were
but a vestige of the great Mississippian chiefdoms that had existed in the
southeastern United States in the last millennium. The story is complex
and I cannot pretend to do justice to the Natchez in this short essay.
Rather, I shall present here a view of what Indian lifeways were like in
the Natchez region in historic times and how that had changed from what

8

existed but a century or so earlier. As archaeology has contributed much to our understanding of the Natchez Indians over the past twenty-five years, I will draw from this rich resource in presenting the story.

The Natchez Elite

Eighteenth-century French adventurers in Louisiana were enamored of the Natchez. Penigaut, Le Page du Pratz, Dumont de Montigny and others wrote of many tribes in their accounts of Indian life in the Mississippi Valley, but it was the Natchez who were their prime focus.[3] Louis XIV considered himself to be *le Roi de Soleil*, but here perched high on the bluffs of the Mississippi River, looking down on all other peoples, was an Indian society that had a Sun King of its own. Not only was the Natchez's complex political structure of interest to these early French adventurers, but so too were their religion, economy, and marriage customs, topics that continue to intrigue twentieth-century anthropologists.[4]

In addition to written accounts, a few Frenchmen also made pictorial records of the eighteenth-century Natchez elite. A portrait of what is thought to be a Natchez Indian was created by Alexandre De Batz. In one corner of a busy scene that depicts Choctaw warriors bearing scalps, De Batz drew a very distinctive individual (fig. 1). Although he is dressed in a European-style shirt, he is clearly an Indian as he wears an elaborate feather crown and has a painted face. The Great Sun of the Natchez was reported to have worn such a headdress,[5] so it has been thought by some that this particular individual may in fact have been a Natchez chief.

It is possible that De Batz may have provided sketches to Le Page du Pratz, for the engravings that accompany the text in Le Page's major treatise bear stylistic similarities with De Batz's work.[6] There is one image in this volume that has become synonymous with the Natchez. In Figure 2 the Great Sun is being carried to the harvest feast. He is raised high above the ground on a litter borne by eight men, a reflection of the regal dimension of Natchezan society. The power exhibited in this sketch is matched only by the scene depicting the mourning ceremony of the Tattooed Serpent, principal war chief of the Natchez and brother of the Great Sun (fig. 3). When his brother died in 1725 the Great Sun was so distraught that he made plans to end his own life, but because the loss of such an important ally would have been a crushing blow to the French, they persuaded him not to do so. His reconsideration was fortunate for the Natchez themselves, not only because they would have lost a beloved leader, but because the death of a Sun demanded human sacrifice. It was

Fig. 1. Possibly a Natchez Sun (chief) of the early eighteenth century.
Detail from a drawing by Alexandre De Batz entitled, "Sauvages Tchaktas Matachez en Guerriers qui portent des Chevelures." Courtesy of the Peabody Museum, Harvard University. Photograph by Hillel Burger. Neg. no. N31908; Cat. no. 42-70-10/19.

Fig. 2. The Great Sun being carried on a litter.
Reproduced from Le Page du Pratz, *Histoire de la Louisiane*, 2:facing 367. Photograph by Hillel Burger.

10

Fig. 3. Mortuary ceremony of the Tattooed Serpent, brother of the Great Sun.
Reproduced from Le Page du Pratz, *Histoire de la Louisiane*, 3:facing 55. Photograph by Hillel Burger.

unthinkable for a member of the Sun family to go into the afterlife alone; therefore a number of individuals had to die also to serve as retainers.

Eight people are in the process of being sacrificed in the Tattooed Serpent's mourning ceremony. Each sitting individual has a cord wrapped around his or her neck, the ends of which are held in the hands of a close relative. At some time during the event, a plug of tobacco will be swallowed by the victims, thus dazing them and reducing their awareness of the tightening cords. As the funeral litter travels in slow circles before the temple, sacrificed babies will be thrown on the ground by their parents to be trampled by the procession. To be sacrificed in such a monumental event was considered a great honor, and the victims usually went willingly, because their deaths elevated the status of their families. The "Stinkard" (French term for a Natchez commoner) parents who offered their infants were therefore considered "Honored" people. [7]

The Historic Grand Village and
Secondary Ceremonial Centers

The temple before which the Tattooed Serpent's mortuary ceremony occurred was located at the Fatherland site, Grand Village of the Natchez Indians (figs. 4 and 5). Nestled in a curve of St. Catherine Creek, the Grand Village was the focus of considerable activity in the early contact between French and Indians. Probably two of the three extant mounds at the site were actually in use in the late seventeenth and early eighteenth centuries. One (Mound B) supported the chief's house, whereas the other smaller tumulus (Mound C) was the foundation for the temple.

Moreau B. Chambers conducted the first professional excavations at Fatherland in 1930, work that was later reported on by James A. Ford. Several Indian burials were found in the upper levels of Mound C, many of which contained European trade goods. Robert S. Neitzel (fig. 6), in his role as Mississippi state archaeologist, completely excavated Mounds B and C in the early 1960s. Both mounds exhibited multiple building stages bearing nearly identical floor plans from top to bottom, an indication that these same functions (chief's house and temple) existed far back into prehistory. It is now known that the Fatherland site began its long service as a ceremonial center for the Natchez Indians around A.D. 1350. [8]

Ceremonial center is a standard archaeological term. It basically means the location where the elite resided, a central meeting ground for the society at certain times of the year. As various social events oc-

12

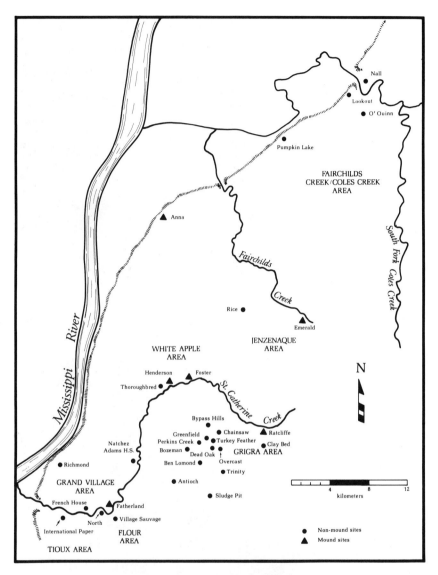

Fig. 4. Historic and Protohistoric Sites in the Natchez region.
Reproduced from Brown, *Natchez Indian Archaeology,* Fig. 3. Courtesy of the Mississippi Department of Archives and History. Drawing by Nancy Lambert-Brown.

Fig. 5. Robert S. Neitzel's 1962 excavations in the temple mound (Md. C) at Fatherland. Note the ramp leading up to the summit.
Courtesy of the Lower Mississippi Survey, Peabody Museum. Photograph by Stephen Williams. Neg. no. 62/22.

Fig. 6. Robert S. Neitzel, "Great Sun" of Southeastern archaeology, and Archie Sam, a twentieth century chief of the Natchez Indians.
Reproduced from a slide. Photograph by Robert Wilson.

14

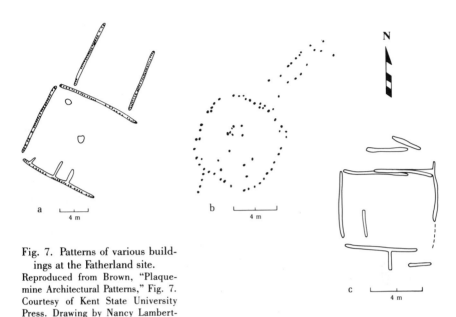

a L___I___I 4 m   b L___I___I 4 m   N

Fig. 7. Patterns of various build-
ings at the Fatherland site.
Reproduced from Brown, "Plaque-
mine Architectural Patterns," Fig. 7.
Courtesy of Kent State University
Press. Drawing by Nancy Lambert-
Brown.

c L___I___I 4 m

curred, the population would gravitate to ceremonial centers. For much
of the year, however, these locations might be vacant or have only a small
resident population, perhaps the elite and their servants. This was
certainly the case at the Grand Village. One of the prime goals of
Neitzel's 1972 excavations at the Fatherland site was to find houses
between and around the mounds.[9] Although he did indeed find some
architectural patterns indicative of residence at the site (fig. 7), the
actual number of houses found is significantly small.

Most of the Natchez Indians resided in small villages known as
hamlets, which were widely distributed throughout the region. Archaeology suggests that in many locales there were even smaller residential
communities of perhaps one or two houses. All of these settlements were
linked with various ceremonial centers. The Grand Village was the
principal one in historic times, but there were perhaps as many as eight
others in the region that supported second-level members of the Sun
family.[10]

A good example of a secondary ceremonial center is the Foster site,
located on the north bank of St. Catherine Creek in the vicinity of
present-day Washington, Mississippi. There are two mounds at the site,
the largest one (A) being clearly visible; it supports a modern building

15

on its summit. Directly to the south is a much smaller mound (B) hidden in a clump of trees. Excavations were conducted at this site in 1971–1972 by Jeffrey P. Brain of Harvard University's Lower Mississippi Survey (LMS). Although Brain did not detect evidence of historic occupation, probably because of mound erosion, he did uncover an extremely important protohistoric (sixteenth–seventeenth-century) component.

Local lore has it that the historic White Apple Village, which figured so importantly in the Natchez Massacre of 1729 as well as in earlier confrontations with the French, was located south of Natchez along the west bank of Second Creek. However, on the basis of literature research, cartographic analysis, and archaeological investigation, we may now say that White Apple almost certainly existed in the general vicinity of the Foster site. Foster may, in fact, have been the ceremonial center for this village.[11] So how then did the Mazique site on Second Creek (not on fig. 4) become associated with White Apple?

Joseph Frank has argued that the designation of the Mazique site as White Apple began as early as 1772 when Anthony Hutchins recorded it as such. Apparently a Natchez Indian had lived in the vicinity of this site in the late eighteenth century, an Indian who could have been an inhabitant of the original White Apple Village.[12] The myth of the Mazique/White Apple equivalence was perpetuated by a museum that was erected on the property in the 1930s, the remains of which are still quite visible to all who travel along U.S. 61. The three mounds at the site are still there, too, but are difficult to see because of vegetation.

In an early survey of the Mazique site James Ford collected Indian pottery from the fields, most of which has been securely dated to the period A.D. 800–1000. But the discovery of a white clay tobacco pipe fragment and of a shard of Fatherland Incised, *var. Fatherland*, in Ford's collection certainly suggests an early eighteenth-century occupation as well. Since Ford is also reported to have found a gunflint at Mazique, a historic component cannot be ruled out.[13] Although there has never been a professional excavation at Mazique, John L. Cotter and W. P. Lancaster, archaeologists with the National Park Service, did intensively survey the site in 1948. They investigated a trench that earlier had been cut through the middle of the largest mound below its base. At the bottom of this trench they observed a thick midden layer, the garbage of a premound village. Contained in this layer was pottery that dates after A.D. 1400 and could even date as late as protohistoric times. Without further excavation, it is impossible to say just when the mounds at

16

Mazique were constructed, but it is now clear that they were a late prehistoric phenomenon broadly contemporary with mound construction at Fatherland.

Emerald and Anna: Major Ceremonial Centers
of the Late Prehistoric Natchez

Somewhere in the vicinity of the Emerald site (fig. 8), located at the southern end of the Natchez Trace, the village of Jenzenaque existed in historic times. The ceremonial center for this village may even have been located at Emerald itself. Emerald was definitely the most important Natchez site in the protohistoric period, of far greater significance than Fatherland ever was.[14] This magnificent edifice, the second-largest (bulkiest) late prehistoric mound site in North America, once supported a chiefly society that was second to none in this portion of Mississippi.

Once known as the Selsertown Mound, the Emerald site has been in the archaeological literature for over 150 years. It was the scene of many a "picnic trip" by nineteenth-century learned societies.[15] Although stabilization work conducted by the National Park Service in 1955 modified the site somewhat, giving it a carefully manicured appearance, it is clear from contour maps made in the past that the restoration has been faithful to its original appearance. The base mound, which rises thirty feet from the ground surface along its edge, has an extensive platform that measures approximately five acres. At one time there were eight mounds arranged around the border of this platform. The largest mound (fig. 9), situated on the western end, rises an additional thirty feet above the platform. Anyone who stands on top of this tumulus has a commanding view of the countryside, certainly an appropriate location for a Great Sun. Directly opposite, on the eastern end of the platform, is the next-largest mound (B). Six additional tumuli were arranged around the edge of the platform, three to a side. The designers of this magnificent earthwork wisely took advantage of a natural hill in their plan. To form the base mound, they piled soil around the edge of this hill to create a platform. The smaller mounds obviously were added later. Considering that there were no draught animals in prehistoric times and everything had to be carried on human backs, the erection of the Emerald site was an impressive feat. Multiple child burials found in the excavation of Mound B perhaps hark back to an early mortuary ceremony of a high-ranked individual.[16]

A site that bears many parallels with Emerald as an overall site plan is the Anna site (fig. 8). A total of eight pyramidal mounds occurs at this

Anna

Emerald

Fig. 8. Comparison of site plans at Anna and Emerald.
Reproduced from Brain, "Late Prehistoric Settlement Patterning," Fig. 12.6. Courtesy of the author and Academic Press.

site. Six of them are arranged in a cluster on a high bluff overlooking the Mississippi Valley; two others are positioned on nearby knolls. As with the Emerald site, the principal mound at Anna is located along the western edge of the site. It is about fifty-four feet tall and has a well-preserved ramp that faces east-southeast to the next-largest mound. Smaller tumuli are arranged around the edge of the plaza formed by the two large mounds, reminiscent of the pattern at Emerald.[17]

The principal difference between Anna and Emerald is that the secondary mounds at Anna were built on a natural bluff top. The builders of Emerald created an artificial bluff top in their construction of the platform mound, and then put the secondary mounds on top. It is significant though that the major axes of the two sites run along cardinal directions. In both cases the highest mound, which probably supported the home of the highest-ranked Sun, occurs on the west. As this person rose each morning he faced toward his relative, the rising sun.

Equally interesting is the timing of mound construction at the two sites. Archaeological investigations show that at least one of the Anna mounds (No. 5) had most of its construction undertaken between A.D. 1200 and 1500. The Emerald site occupation overlaps with Anna, but mound construction at Emerald continued throughout the sixteenth and early seventeenth centuries, long after Anna's heyday. Anna came into being at a time when sociopolitical activity seems to have been more oriented to the Mississippi River. The shift of power to Emerald perhaps symbolizes a reorientation of Natchezan society to the interior. The positioning of Emerald adjacent to the Natchez Trace may be more than coincidental. Why such a shift should have taken place is not known, but it is clear that the people who occupied Anna and Emerald were closely related, if not the same. We know this to be true, because they not only continued to make the same pottery (prime evidence for determining relationships), but they carried their site plan with them, even to the extent of creating a high bluff to maintain the Great Sun in his appropriate position.[18]

Stability in the Face of Change

Archaeologists can say much about what events occurred and when, but explanations for why are harder to come by. The residents of Anna and Emerald once ruled over a large territory stretching from Vicksburg in the north to the Homochitto River in the south. Its constituents probably numbered in the thousands, compared to the hundreds in historic times. De Soto's army experienced the power of the prehistoric

Natchez in their contact with the nation that was then called Quigualtam. When De Soto demanded that their chief come to see him, he received a response that is worthy of a Natchezan Great Sun:

> As to what you say of your being the son of the Sun, if you will cause him to dry up the great river, I will believe you: as to the rest, it is not my custom to visit any one, but rather all, of whom I have ever heard, have come to visit me, to serve and obey me, and pay me tribute, either voluntarily or by force: if you desire to see me, come where I am; if for peace, I will receive you with special goodwill; if for war, I will await you in my town; but neither for you, nor for any man, will I set back one foot.[19]

De Soto did not live to humble this chief, but his army discovered that any attempt to have done so would have resulted in failure. As the remnants of de Soto's forces floated down the Mississippi River in their makeshift vessels, they were repeatedly attacked from boats by a multitude of warriors from the Quigualtam Nation. The Spaniards were no match for such a manifestation of power. A century-and-a-half later this same society, the Natchez that La Salle met in his 1682 travels on the Mississippi, were certainly not the Quigualtam of de Soto's time. They were their descendants, to be sure, and they still controlled this portion of Mississippi, but their power had been severely diminished.[20]

Diseases spread throughout the southeastern region in the wake of the Spanish, and the Natchez were but one of a number of important groups that experienced major demographic changes in the late sixteenth and seventeenth centuries.[21] Such major ceremonial centers as Anna and Emerald (fig. 9) still rose high above the landscape, but the trees now grew thick on the sides of the mounds. An elite continued to survive; there was still a Sun family, but their glamor and power were severely reduced. It was between the periods of de Soto and La Salle that the focus of Natchezan society shifted to the Fatherland site, and it was also at this time that intruders started to enter the area. These intruders, however, were Indians, and, unlike the Spanish, they were welcome.

The Yazoo Basin, immediately north of Natchezan territory, had societies that were probably even more impressive than that of Quigualtam in late prehistoric times, but by the time the French moved into the Mississippi Valley in the late sixteenth century, the Yazoo Basin was all but abandoned. The major populations had been reduced to a scattering of Indian villages nestled along the bluffs overlooking the Yazoo River. Some of these remnant populations, such as the Grigra and Tioux, traveled even farther south and settled among the Natchez. Adopting

Fig. 9. The Lower Mississippi Survey's 1972 excavations at Emerald.
Reproduced from a slide. Courtesy of the Lower Mississippi Survey, Peabody Museum.

these people was one way the Natchez managed to bring new blood into their society, which had been severely reduced by the diseases that passed up and down the valley in post-de Soto times.[22]

Some of these adopted people settled along the lower reaches of St. Catherine Creek; some moved into the rugged area north of what is now Liberty Road; and others are believed to have settled north of Natchez where Coles Creek emerges from the bluffs. Many of the sites in these areas have been excavated by Lower Mississippi Survey groups in the 1970s and 1980s.[23] As a result of these investigations, we have learned much about the material culture, settlement patterns, and mortuary behavior of both indigenous Natchez peoples and adopted groups. Such sites as Ratcliffe and Foster have yielded information on second-level ceremonial centers; O'Quinn, Rice, and North have provided useful data on how the "Stinkards" buried their dead; and Village Sauvage, Antioch, Greenfield, Trinity, and Lookout have shown what life in the hamlets was like. Although these investigations have greatly enhanced knowledge of lifeways in the Natchez region, the story is still far from complete. To unravel the complex cultural developments which occurred in this area over time, and especially during the dynamic seventeenth and eighteenth centuries, much more intensive excavations are required.

The Lookout site demonstrates just how complex the story can be. This nonmound village site was excavated in 1981–1982. Figure 10 displays the foundations of four distinct buildings that were uncovered: a large circular one made of individually set posts, and three rectangular ones whose vertical members were placed in wall trenches. Obviously these buildings were not occupied at the same time, for the walls are overlapping. The circular one probably dates from A.D. 1000–1200, whereas the others were erected at different times between A.D. 1200–1680.[24] Lookout is a typical situation in Natchez—the reoccupation of sites over many centuries. Such reuse complicates archaeological reconstruction, making it difficult to determine which people built which structures.

European lead-glazed earthenware and historic Indian pottery at the Lookout site indicate that this site was used as late as the French occupation of Natchez. The very crude sandstone effigy pipe found at Lookout could date to this period or to a slightly earlier time (fig. 11). The pipe bears a simple serpentine design on one side and a human face on its end. It is a far cry from the elaborate limestone pipes that were once smoked by the elite of Emerald (fig. 12). Although clearly representing a human face, the sculpture on the Lookout pipe lacks the realism manifested in the famous stone figure from Natchez (fig. 13).

This effigy, made of sandstone, once belonged to Joseph Thompson of Natchez. He is reported to have found it in the 1790s on land where an Indian temple had stood, perhaps the Fatherland site. Although it is plain compared to sculptural work done by Mississippian populations several centuries earlier, it was probably extremely important to the Natchez. Stone and clay human effigies such as this one are known to have been kept in the temples of the Natchez and Taensa Indians. They were important religious objects closely identified with the Natchez hierarchy. In fact, the Natchez themselves believed their Suns were spirits that had descended from such effigies.[25] Thompson gave this pipe to Winthrop Sargent, and Sargent donated it to the American Antiquarian Society in 1817. It came to the Peabody Museum in 1910, and since then has inspired the many operations of the Lower Mississippi Survey. It is a constant reminder of the rich and colorful cultural heritage of Natchez long before the nineteenth century.

It is possible that a few Natchez Indians remained in the area following their confrontations with the French in 1729–1730, but most of them left. Some traveled west for a short period, settling in the vicinity of Sicily Island, Louisiana, but they were soon brought to their knees by

Fig. 10. Building patterns at the Lookout site.
Reproduced from Brown, *Natchez Indian Archaeology*, Fig. 17. Courtesy of the Mississippi Department of Archives and History. Photograph by Ian W. Brown.

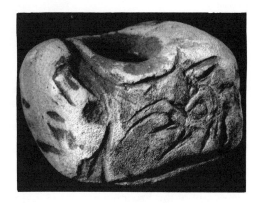

Fig. 11. Sandstone pipe from the Lookout site, with a degenerate feathered serpent pattern on its side and a human face on its end. Length, 3¼ in.
Courtesy of the Peabody Museum, Harvard University. Gift of Robert Prospere of Natchez. Photograph by Hillel Burger. Neg. no. N31906; Cat no. 980-14-10/58238.

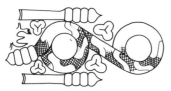

Fig. 12. One of the famous Perrault pipes from Emerald. Length, 4¾ in.
Reproduced from Philip Phillips and James A. Brown, *Pre-Columbian Shell Engravings from the Craig Mound at Spiro, Oklahoma*, 6 vols. (Cambridge: Peabody Museum Press, 1978, 1984), 1: Fig. 267. Courtesy of the authors and the Peabody Museum, Harvard University.

Fig. 13. Human effigy of sandstone found in Natchez in the 1790s. Height, 16 in.
Courtesy of the Peabody Museum, Harvard University. Photograph by Hillel Burger. Neg. no. N31907e; Cat. no. 10-47-10/79934.

the weight of the French empire and its Indian allies. These remnants of the once-great Natchez Nation were transported to the West Indies where they were reduced to a life of slavery. The remainder joined the Chickasaw, long-time enemies of the French who no doubt valued the addition of Natchez warriors to their ranks. Over the years small splinter groups of Natchez appeared in a number of areas among different southeastern groups, particularly the Upper Creeks of Alabama. Eventually, like most of their neighbors, they were driven west to Indian territory by Andrew Jackson and his supporters in the third decade of the nineteenth century.

Although the Natchez left the area many years ago, their earthworks were built to survive the ages. The multiple layers of soil, followed by caps of clay and successive episodes of burning were intended to defy nature. And that they did, but the mounds cannot withstand the onslaught of twentieth-century society. What took years to build can now, with heavy machinery, be dismantled in hours. Natchez has indeed a proud past. The city is based on a solid foundation of enormous cultural achievement by its Indian predecessors. One hopes these achievements will be appreciated before it is too late. Emerald, Anna, and a few additional sites certainly will survive into the twenty-first century, but unless a major effort is made by the city to preserve and protect its archaeological sites, this last source of information on the Natchez will cease to exist.

Archaeological Sites: Lower Mississippi Survey Numbers

Anna (26-K-1)

Antioch (26-K-100)

Ben Lomond (26-K-101)

Bozeman (26-K-48)

Bypass Hills (26-K-129)

Chainsaw (26-K-110)

Clay Bed (26-K-120)

Dead Oak (26-K-104)

Emerald (26-L-1)

Fatherland (26-K-2)

Foster (26-K-3)

French House (26-K-109)

Greenfield (26-K-92)

Henderson (26-K-4)

International Paper (26-K-18)

Lookout (25-L-28)

Mazique (27-K-1)

Nall (25-L-3)

Natchez Adams H.S. (26-K-90)

North (26-K-68)

O'Quinn (25-L-29)

Overcast (26-K-107)

Perkins Creek (26-K-93)

Pumpkin Lake (26-K-88)

Ratcliffe (26-K-46)

Rice (26-K-91)

Richmond (26-K-102)

Sludge Pit (26-K-116)

Thoroughbred (26-K-74)

Trinity (26-K-115)

Turkey Feather (26-K-122)

Village Sauvage (26-K-22)

This essay is dedicated to Leicester McGehee, a man who loved the land as much as any Natchez Indian. I learned much from Leicester, and am indebted to both him and to Miss Betty for their warmth and friendship over the years. I would also like to thank a number of other contemporary Natchezans who have been a source of aid and comfort to numerous Lower Mississippi Survey crews in the past two decades: "Smokye Joe" Frank, Robert and Kathy Prospere, Lee and Sherry Jones, Grace MacNeil, James and Fan Barnett, Ron and Mimi Miller, Logan and Rinza Sewell, Charles and Alice Feltus, and Mayor Tony Byrne. Jeffrey Brain and Stephen Williams read an original draft of this essay and offered much appreciated advice.

Notes

1. The word *Natchez* comes from *Natché*, which was only one of the villages of these people. Jeffrey P. Brain, "La Salle at the Natchez: An Archaeological and Historical Perspective," in Patricia K. Galloway (ed.), *La Salle and His Legacy: Frenchmen and Indians in the Lower Mississippi Valley* (Jackson: University Press of Mississippi, 1982). Their own name for themselves was more like *Thécoel*. For phonetic variations on this name see John R. Swanton, *Indian Tribes of the Lower Mississippi Valley and Adjacent Coast of the Gulf of Mexico*, Bureau of American Ethnology Bulletin, No. 43 (Washington, D.C.: Government Printing Office, 1911), 25, 46–47.

2. The Calusa also had a complex chiefdom, but not on the same level with that of the Natchez. See John M. Goggin and William C. Sturtevant, "The Calusa: A Stratified, Nonagricultural Society (with Notes on Sibling Marriage)," in Ward H. Goodenough (ed.), *Explorations in Cultural Anthropology: Essays in Honor of George Peter Murdock* (New York: McGraw-Hill, 1964), 179–219. Randolph J. Widmer, *The Evolution of the Calusa: A Nonagricultural Chiefdom on the Southwest Florida Coast* (Tuscaloosa and London: The University of Alabama Press, 1988), 3–8.

3. Richebourg G. McWilliams (ed. and trans.), *Fleur de Lys and Calumet: Being the Pénicaut Narrative of French Adventure in Louisiana* (Baton Rouge: Louisiana State University Press, 1953); Antoine S. Le Page du Pratz, *Histoire de la Louisiane* (3 vols.; Paris, 1758); Dumont de Montigny, *Mémoires Historiques sur la Louisiane* (2 vols.; Paris, 1753).

4. John R. Swanton, *Indian Tribes*, 45–257. Although there have been many other contributions on Natchez lifeways since this volume was published, none have surpassed Swanton in the depth of coverage. See also Jeffrey P. Brain, "The Natchez 'Paradox,'" *Ethnology*, 10, No. 2 (1971), 215–22; Douglas R. White, George P. Murdock, and Richard Scaglion, "Natchez Class and Rank Reconsidered," *Ethnology*, 10, No. 4 (1971), 369–88.

5. Swanton, *Indian Tribes*, 106–107; David I. Bushnell, Jr., "Drawings by A. De Batz in Louisiana, 1732–1735," *Smithsonian Miscellaneous Collections*, 80, No. 5 (1927), 11–12.

6. Samuel Wilson, "Louisiana Drawings by Alexandre De Batz," *Journal of the Society of Architectural Historians*, 22, No. 2 (May, 1963), 83.

7. The Natchez mortuary ceremonies existed on a much grander scale before the eighteenth century. As a result of French influences the complex rituals soon began to disintegrate. The number of sacrificial victims had decreased markedly by the time of the Tattooed Serpent's death along with willingness to participate. See Swanton, *Indian Tribes*, 138–57.

8. James A. Ford, *Analysis of Indian Village Site Collections from Louisiana and Mississippi*, Department of Conservation, Louisiana Geological Survey, Anthropology Study, No. 2 (New Orleans: Department of Conservation, 1936), 59–64; Robert S. Neitzel, *Archeology of the Fatherland Site: The Grand Village of the Natchez*, Anthropological Papers of the American Museum of Natural History, 51, Pt. 1 (1965); Ian W. Brown, "Plaquemine Architectural Patterns in the Natchez Bluffs and Surrounding Regions of the Lower Mississippi Valley," *Midcontinental Journal of Archaeology*, 10, No. 2 (1985), 267–72.

9. Robert S. Neitzel, *The Grand Village of the Natchez Revisited: Excavations at the Fatherland Site, Adams County, Mississippi, 1972,* Mississippi Department of Archives and History, Archaeological Report, No. 12 (Jackson: Mississippi Department of Archives and History, 1983), 9.

10. Ian W. Brown, "An Archaeological Study of Culture Contact and Change in the Natchez Bluffs Region," in Galloway (ed.), *La Salle and His Legacy,* 184–85; Ian W. Brown, *Natchez Indian Archaeology: Culture Change and Stability in the Lower Mississippi Valley,* Mississippi Department of Archives and History, Archaeological Report, No. 15 (Jackson: Mississippi Department of Archives and History, 1985), 4, 6.

11. Ford, *Indian Village Site Collections,* 172; Andrew C. Albrecht, "The Location of the Historic Natchez Villages," *Journal of Mississippi History,* 6, No. 2 (1944), 81–82. It is also possible that the nearby Henderson site could have served this same role. See Jeffrey P. Brain, Ian W. Brown, and Vincas P. Steponaitis, "Archaeology of the Natchez Bluffs" (Unpublished MS, Lower Mississippi Survey, Peabody Museum, Cambridge).

12. Joseph V. Frank III, "In Defense of Hutchins' Natchez Indian," *Mississippi Archaeological Association Newsletter,* 10, No. 4 (1975); John F. H. Claiborne, *Mississippi, as a Province, Territory and State, with Biographical Notices of Eminent Citizens* (1 vol.; Jackson: Power and Barksdale, 1880), 48. To add to the confusion, 19 miles east of the Mazique site is a small contemporary village called White Apple. How the naming of this community fits into the story is another unsolved puzzle.

13. Jeffrey P. Brain, interview, March 22, 1988; Ford, *Indian Village Site Collections,* 172. A reanalysis of Ford's collection at Louisiana State University was undertaken by the Lower Mississippi Survey in 1971.

14. Brown, "Archaeological Study of Culture Contact," 184–88; Brown, *Natchez Indian Archaeology,* 4–10; Brain, Brown, and Steponaitis, *Archaeology of the Natchez Bluffs;* John L. Cotter, "Stratigraphic and Area Tests at the Emerald and Anna Mound Sites," *American Antiquity,* 17, No. 1, Pt. 1 (1951), 18–24; William N. Morgan, *Prehistoric Architecture in the Eastern United States* (Cambridge, Mass., and London: MIT Press, 1980), 93.

15. The picnic event was revived by Sherry and H. Lee Jones and the LMS crew in 1982.

16. See Brain, Brown, and Steponaitis, *Archaeology of the Natchez Bluffs,* for details on the 1972 LMS excavations at this site.

17. Morgan, *Prehistoric Architecture,* 92; Cotter, "Stratigraphic and Area Tests," 24–28; Ian W. Brown and Jeffrey P. Brain, "Archaeology of the Natchez Bluffs Region, Mississippi: Hypothesized Cultural and Environmental Factors Influencing Local Population Movements," *Southeastern Archaeological Conference Bulletin,* 20 (1983), 43, 47; Jeffrey P. Brain, "Late Prehistoric Settlement Patterning in the Yazoo Basin and Natchez Bluffs Regions of the Lower Mississippi Valley," in Bruce D. Smith (ed.), *Mississippian Settlement Patterns* (New York: Academic Press, 1978), 347–49.

18. Cotter, "Stratigraphic and Area Tests," 24–28; Brain, Brown, and Steponaitis, *Archaeology of the Natchez Bluffs;* Brown and Brain, "Archaeology of the Natchez Bluffs," 47–48.

19. Edward G. Bourne, *Narratives of the Career of Hernando de Soto* (2 vols.; New York: Allerton, 1922), I, 154–55.

20. Jeffrey P. Brain, "Introduction: Update of de Soto Studies since the United States de Soto Expedition Commission Report," in John R. Swanton, *Final Report of the United*

States de Soto Expedition Commission (Washington, D.C.: Smithsonian Institution Press, 1985), xliii–xlvi; Brain, "The Natchez 'Paradox,'" 219–20; Brain, "La Salle at the Natchez."

21. Henry F. Dobyns, *Their Number Become Thinned: Native American Population Dynamics in Eastern North America* (Knoxville: University of Tennessee Press, 1983); Marvin T. Smith, *Archaeology of Aboriginal Culture Change in the Interior Southeast: Depopulation During the Early Historic Period*, Ripley P. Bullen Monographs in Anthropology and History, No. 6 (Gainesville: University of Florida Press, 1987); Philip Phillips, James A. Ford, and James B. Griffin, *Archaeological Survey in the Lower Mississippi Alluvial Valley, 1940–1947*, Papers of the Peabody Museum of Archaeology and Ethnology, 25 (Cambridge: Peabody Museum, Harvard University, 1951), 419–21; Ann F. Ramenofsky, *Vectors of Death: The Archaeology of European Contact* (Albuquerque: University of New Mexico Press, 1987), 42–71.

22. Brain, "Winterville: A Case Study of Prehistoric Culture Contact in the Lower Mississippi Valley" (Ph.D. dissertation, Yale University, 1969); Brain, "Late Prehistoric Settlement Patterning"; Stephen Williams and Jeffrey P. Brain, *Excavations at the Lake George Site, Yazoo County, Mississippi, 1958–1960*, Papers of the Peabody Museum of Archaeology and Ethnology, 74 (Cambridge: Peabody Museum, Harvard University, 1983); Philip Phillips, *Archaeological Survey in the Lower Yazoo Basin, Mississippi, 1949–1955*, Papers of the Peabody Museum of Archaeology and Ethnology, 60 (Cambridge: Peabody Museum, Harvard University, 1970); Jeffrey P. Brain, *Tunica Archaeology*, Papers of the Peabody Museum of Archaeology and Ethnology, 78 (Cambridge: Peabody Museum, Harvard University, 1988); Patricia K. Galloway, "Historic Tribes in the Yazoo Basin during the French Colonial Period," appendix to Samuel O. Brookes, *Cultural Resources along the Yazoo River from Greenwood to Vicksburg, Mississippi* (Vicksburg: U.S. Army Corps of Engineers, Contract DACW38-81-P-2166, 1982); Ian W. Brown, "Early 18th Century French-Indian Culture Contact in the Yazoo Bluffs Region of the Lower Mississippi Valley" (Ph.D. dissertation, Brown University, 1979); Brain, "The Natchez 'Paradox,'" 219–21; Swanton, *Indian Tribes*, 46–48, 334–36; Brown, "Archaeological Study of Culture Contact," 179, 186–88.

23. Brain, Brown, and Steponaitis, *Archaeology of the Natchez Bluffs*; Brown, *Natchez Indian Archaeology*.

24. Brown, *Natchez Indian Archaeology*, 31–39.

25. Caleb Atwater, "Description of the Antiquities Discovered in the State of Ohio and Other Western States," *Transactions and Collections of the American Antiquarian Society*, 1 (1820), 215; Stephen Williams, *The Waring Papers: The Collected Works of Antonio J. Waring, Jr.*, Papers of the Peabody Museum of Archaeology and Ethnology, 58 (Cambridge: Peabody Museum, Harvard University, 1968), 60–61, Fig. 15; Swanton, *Indian Tribes*, 164, 172. It is possible that this effigy was cached in Md. C at Fatherland at the time of the Natchez Massacre. Since Moreau B. Chambers also discovered a rich amount of native and European items just beneath the surface of this mound, there is an implication that the Natchez may have hastily buried some of their treasures before leaving the area. Stephen Williams, interview, March 22, 1988; Neitzel, "Archeology of the Fatherland Site," plates 8–9.

Natchez in French Louisiana and Chateaubriand's Epic, *The Natchez*

LETHA WOOD AUDHUY

If you mention Natchez to the average French person today, chances are you will meet a pause, a moment of reflection, and then something like this: "Natchez . . .? Oh, yes: the Indians, *Atala*, Chateaubriand!" as if the word resonated in his memories of school days, evoking vague and flowery images of the great "Méschacébé." Over the past year and a half, while attempting to determine what place Natchez holds in French history and literature, I have entered the labyrinth of the various French archives and libraries to look for the records about a settlement in the French colony of Louisiana in the early 18th century, and have been captivated by François-René de Chateaubriand's dramatic and romantic tale entitled *The Natchez*, a prose poem centering on the Natchez massacre of 1729, published in 1827, which may be the ultimate source of the "average" Frenchman's vague knowledge of Natchez, and almost certainly is responsible for his association of Natchez with Chateaubriand.[1]

Why did Chateaubriand write about that episode? In *Les Mémoires d'Outre-Tombe* he explained:

> I was still young when I conceived the idea of making an epic about man in nature or painting the manners of the savages by linking them to some well-known event. After the discovery of America, I could see no more interesting subject, especially to the French, than the massacre of the Natchez colony in Louisiana in 1727 [*sic*]. All the Indian tribes conspiring after two centuries of oppression to give liberty back to the New World seemed to me to offer a subject almost as auspicious as the Conquest of Mexico. I jotted down some

29

fragments of this work on paper; but I soon realized that I lacked the true colors, and if I wanted to make a picture of what it was like, I had to visit, as Homer did, the peoples I wanted to paint.[2]

However, there are other indications, first, that this was a kind of *a posteriori* justification, and, second, that Chateaubriand's original idea was to write a *Canadian* epic.[3] In any case, it is certain that Chateaubriand, at age twenty-three, went off to America to gather material, and that he spent five months there in 1791, from July 10 to December 10. Throughout his voluminous work he never varied in his account of the first part of his trip; he landed in Baltimore, proceeded to Philadelphia, New York, and Boston, went back to New York, and then up the Hudson to Niagara Falls by the Iroquois Trail, and then back to Philadelphia, meeting with various Indians along the way.

Did he actually visit Natchez on the Mississippi? This is a famous and passionate literary controversy, in the course of which Chateaubriand has been mocked for saying he had traveled through the American forests as far as Florida; critics point out that he certainly could not have done this in the summer, accoutred, as he said he was, in bearskins. He suggests in the preface to *Atala* (part of *The Natchez* published in 1801), in *Le Génie du Christianisme* (1802), and in *Le Voyage en Amérique* (1827), an immense but vague itinerary through the South where he "had wandered on the shores of the Mississippi that formed the magnificent southern boundaries of New France"; and, in an unpublished fragment of the *Mémoires* found by J. Bédier, he specifically claims to have "stopped at the Natchez in 1791."[4]

For several reasons, however, it seems highly unlikely, if not impossible, that Chateaubriand ever went down the Mississippi and put in at Natchez. As various French specialists have wondered, how could anyone, even Daniel Boone, in five months (actually in much less time than that, if one accepts Chateaubriand's account of the first part of his trip as far as the Great Lakes) have covered the United States from Niagara Falls to Louisiana and back to Philadelphia, at a time when the Indians were on the warpath, when a general revolt seemed imminent in the Old Northwest, and when communications on the Mississippi were cut off?[5] Most likely, Chateaubriand's testimony that he had traveled on the shores of the Mississippi was simply a belated claim on his readers' credibility, a claim for the verisimilitude of *The Natchez*, published thirty-six years after his journey.

The facts about the composition and publication of *The Natchez* are almost as astonishing as the idea of the bearskin costume in Indian summer. In the preface to *The Natchez*, Chateaubriand claims to have brought with him "the original manuscript" on his return to France in 1791; this was probably *Atala*, written, as he said in the preface, in 1801, "in the wilderness, in the huts of the savages." He soon joined the émigrés in exile in London, in 1793, and began writing or rewriting *The Natchez*. After eight years in England, he returned to France in 1800 leaving a manuscript of 2,393 pages in a trunk with his landlady, taking to France only two episodes, detached from the main work, which would be published as *Atala* in 1801, and *René* in 1803. Almost incredibly, and by extreme good luck and the perseverance of some friends, in 1816 he was able to recover the manuscript left in the trunk in England; he thus set to work again, twenty years later, revising and finishing his work. *The Natchez* was finally published in 1827—the same year as James Fenimore Cooper's *The Prairie*, a work similar in inspiration and theme.

Just as Cooper never went west of the Mississippi, Chateaubriand never went south of the Ohio. Yet, although he was ridiculed for such local color as bears staggering through the woods drunk from eating grapes, a close study of the best authorities of his day reveals that Chateaubriand was perfectly faithful to his sources. It must not be forgotten that he spent eight years in England and there had access to works written in English as well as in French. So for his setting, for Indian customs, and for the historical episode of the Natchez massacre, including the names of some of the principals, the correspondence between history and fiction is very close. The primary sources the author transposed were travelers' narratives—that is, the accounts of missionaries and officers, and the studies of naturalists and geographers. We can cite: in French, Father Charlevoix's *Histoire et Description de la Nouvelle France* (1744), Dumont de Montigny's *Mémoires historiques sur la Louisiane*, set down by Le Mascrier (1753), Le Page du Pratz's *Histoire de la Louisiane* (1758), Father Lafitau's *Moeurs des sauvages américaines comparé aux moeurs des premiers temps* (1724), and Baron de Lafontan's *Voyages en Amérique du Nord* (1728); in English, the American naturalist William Bartram's *Travels Through North and South Carolina* (1791), Jonathan Carver's *Travels to the Interior Parts of America* (1778), and the geographer Gilbert Imlay's *A Topographical Description of the Western Territory of North America* (1792). In his preface, Chateaubriand wrote: "It was from this particular action related by the historian that I made, by enlarging upon it, the subject of my work. The reader will see what fiction added to reality."

As for "reality" or history, one should recapitulate what actually happened at Natchez, in order better to appreciate Chateaubriand's fictional vision. Hernando de Soto went up the Mississippi River in 1541, but it was only when Robert Cavelier, Sieur de la Salle, explored the lower Mississippi Valley and reached the mouth in the spring of 1682 that the history of French Louisiana began. La Salle claimed the whole Mississippi Delta as a possession of France, giving these lands the name of Louisiana in honor of Louis XIV. The court decided to create a colony in 1698—a new El Dorado? Comte de Pontchartrain, the French Minister of the Navy, sent Pierre Le Moyne, Sieur d'Iberville, to establish a settlement in this rich valley. He explored the lower Mississippi in 1699 and went as far north as Natchez in 1700, but the first settlements were on the Gulf, at Biloxi and Dauphin Island. Iberville's brother, Jean-Baptiste Le Moyne, Sieur de Bienville, became the governor of Louisiana and served from 1701 to 1713 and twice again in later years.

In 1712 Antoine Crozat got a charter and became the proprietor of the colony that had only two hundred or three hundred inhabitants. After bankrupting himself and Louisiana, he relinquished the charter in 1717 to the Company of the West, with the famous financier John Law as head. Two years later there was a merger of all French trading and colonizing companies and the Company of the Indies was formed and given exclusive rights in Louisiana; it was to give up all rights to the king (Louis XV) in 1731.

The first Frenchmen in Louisiana were missionaries, soldiers, sailors, and *coureurs de bois* (fur traders) who were in constant contact with the Indians. One of the greatest problems was the lack of farmers. The settlements were isolated, poorly supplied, and agriculture was slow to start. Such internal problems as famine were compounded by the international situation: France was at war (1702–1712); the English were always threatening to extend their influence westward; and there was a constant struggle for influence over the different Indian tribes, not to mention uneasy relations with the Spanish to the east and southwest. The Company of the Indies tried to strengthen the colony, principally by peopling it with slaves to work on the plantations, and then by luring settlers from France; but many of these were in fact deported vagabonds, beggars, convicts, and libertines (as in *Manon Lescaut*). At the height of the "Mississippi Bubble" (1719–1720), the contrast between the enthusiastic "Louisiana Fever" and propaganda about a "Pays de Cocagne," and, on the other hand, the disorder and misery that in fact reigned, was absolute. However, in spite of some setbacks, the colony survived, with

New Orleans (founded in 1722) as its capital, and by 1740 there was still a population of 2,500 whites and 4,500 slaves. In 1763, at the end of the French and Indian War, the French lost Louisiana to the Spanish, and the territory east of the Mississippi River—the present state of Mississippi—to the British.

From early times, the French were fascinated with the site of Natchez. When Iberville stopped there on his second voyage, he said the undulating country, with its green hills sprinkled with groves of trees, reminded him of the French countryside. At the same time the author of *The Pénicaut Narrative* was struck with the manners of the savages: "Of all the savages they are the most civilized nation . . . the nation that has seemed to me the most courteous and civil along the banks of the Mississippi."[6]

In 1701 Sieur de Sauvole, who had been left in charge of the first settlement at Fort Maurepas, had sent four men to the Natchez area "to discover whether the country is good." They said it was "perfectly good and agreeable." Certainly the only Frenchman who disagreed with the general concensus that Natchez should indeed be one day the seat of the colony was Crozat's governor, Antoine de la Mothe Cadillac. When Crozat decided to have a trading post and magazines built at Natchez landing in 1712, la Mothe Cadillac tried to discourage the La Loire brothers, holding that "one might as well try to take the moon with one's teeth as send boats up there"; moreover, the land was worth "absolutely nothing" and "would never produce anything worth speaking about."[7]

Although the French had been well received at first, the Natchez were soon antagonized by the construction of the French trading post on their lands and by Governor de la Mothe Cadillac's refusal to smoke the calumet on one occasion; in retaliation they murdered several French traders and looted the trading post. Bienville, in command of Mississippi, demanded satisfaction, and obtained the execution of the perpetrators (or at least of some Indians), the return of the stolen merchandise, horses, and slaves, and the construction by the Natchez of a fort to be occupied by the French. These events took place in 1714 and 1715.

The construction of Fort Rosalie (named for Countess de Pontchartrain), done by order of the king in 1716, opened the area to French settlement. There were no problems of disease or floods or sterile lands, and tobacco and indigo would grow there. By 1729 the number of inhabitants had increased to more than 750, and the post, with the seven

Natchez villages grouped around it, offered an image of prosperity. At this time, Louisiana was divided into nine administrative districts, and Fort Rosalie was made the headquarters of the new Natchez District.[8]

Unfortunately, trouble erupted again between the French and the Indians into what has been called the Second Natchez War. The French complained of the Natchez's arrogance, shrewdness, independence, and, more particularly, of thefts; the savages strongly resisted French missionaries' attempts to make them adopt the Christian faith and morals, and objected to the French encroachment on their lands and especially on their sacred village on St. Catherine Creek. Earlier, French authorities predicted that only annihilation would remove the problem. In 1722 they made war. The French, with five hundred troops and Bienville at their head, destroyed two villages and then dictated peace again.[9]

However, British intrigue had turned the savages against the French, and a real revolt was to break out at the first occasion. The commander of the fort at Natchez, Captain d'Etcheparre, by all accounts brutal and intransigent, furnished the pretext for what was supposed to be a general Indian uprising in the Mississippi region, and for what was in fact the Natchez massacre. The "violent and covetous" d'Etcheparre, the author of "crying injustices" and "unheard-of exactions" (a tribute of grain to be brought monthly), behaved "like a tyrant."[10] He was even tried by the conseil supérieur for abuse of power, but Governor Etienne Périer pardoned him. Since the best lands had already been taken, he planned to take for himself the land occupied by the Natchez village of Pomme Blanche (White Apple), and he ordered the Indians to vacate them immediately. He only gave them two months to carry out his orders. The Indians' revolt was the only way out, and the neighboring tribes joined the conspiracy. They planned for all tribes to fall upon the French in their districts on the same day late in 1729, in order to eliminate the French from east of the Mississippi. The Choctaws joined with the most alacrity; the Yazoos came in later.[11]

Who were the real instigators of the general revolt? It is a controversial question. The French blamed the Chickasaws and the British dissimulated behind them in the Carolinas. Remarks made by Natchez Indians after the massacre supported that view. Also, the Carolinian James Adair, who went to live with the Indians in 1735, met several old Natchez who told him that the Chickasaws, informed of the Natchez's grievances, at the British traders' advice sent pipes and tobacco to urge them to rise.[12] But the Natchez certainly led the conspiracy.

The French were forewarned of impending trouble, but the presumptuous d'Etcheparre refused to believe either the mother of the Great Sun, who warned him, or several settlers whose Indian mistresses had given away the plot. Meanwhile, the Indians convinced the slaves that they would be freed and could, in turn, enslave the French settlers.

On the morning of November 28, 1729, the Great Sun went to the fort to deliver the monthly provisions that had been exacted, and the Natchez spread out on different pretexts, borrowing guns as if for a hunt. At a signal, they slaughtered the French everywhere at once. Nearly three hundred Frenchmen were killed before noon, and the Great Sun sat in the storehouse counting their heads as they piled up before him. There were only a few male survivors: one soldier, about twenty planters who swam across the Mississippi, and a carter and a tailor, who were put to work carrying away the loot and altering French clothes for the Indians.[13] The Indians captured more than four hundred women and children; they planned to "use" them or sell them into slavery. The most flourishing settlement in Louisiana was thus ruined—an irreparable blow to the French colony.

The Natchez massacre was followed soon afterward by a massacre at Fort St. Claude, perpetrated by the Yazoos, but the general uprising did not occur. Why did the Natchez thus anticipate the other tribes and cause the conspiracy to fail? In this case, historical truth offers a picturesque explanation, scarcely to be embroidered upon by Chateaubriand: Antoine Simon Le Page du Pratz, the historian and officer, who took part in the punitive expedition against the Natchez, was told by the mother of the Great Sun herself that the chiefs had distributed sticks in equal number to each tribe, agreeing to burn one each day until there were no more, giving the signal of the uprising; in hopes of saving some Frenchmen she herself withdrew a few sticks from the bundle in the temple, thus starting the insurrection early.[14] The French were then on the defensive, and it was impossible for other tribes to attack.

Aided by the Choctaws, the French arrived at the Natchez on February 8, 1730, and laid siege. The Indians impaled some of the French children on the palisades, a monstrous act that gave the inexperienced French troops courage to attack, as Le Page du Pratz observes. Finally, the Natchez released their prisoners to the Choctaws, who gave them up to the French. The Natchez themselves fled. Chevalier de Louboey had the Natchez forts razed, a new fortress built on the site of Fort Rosalie and occupied by a garrison of 120 men. The Indians continued to make raids; when the Company of the Indies sent reinforcements from France, Governor Périer launched a new expedition to search for the Natchez and crush them. The Natchez capitulated on January 24, 1731, or, rather, 450 women and children and 45 warriors did. These were sold into slavery at Santo Domingo; several hundred others escaped and took refuge with the Chickasaws. "Thus was destroyed this nation, formerly the most brilliant in the colony and the most useful to the French," Le Page du Pratz said.[15] This episode coincided with the end of Law's and the Company of the Indies' administration of Louisiana, and in fact dealt the coup de grâce to it. The company ceded Louisiana to the king, and for the rest of its French history, it was a royal colony.

As John Ray Skates says, there was no way to revive the Natchez settlement, which seemed to be cursed and haunted by the spirits of the massacre. Only a few French soldiers remained there, "on outpost duty in a decaying fort," until 1763, when Natchez was turned over to the British (who had had their eyes on it for years). Thus, the massacre ended French influence in Mississippi.[16]

If the events at Natchez were only an anecdote in history, in literature they were to assume epic, even mythical dimensions as Chateaubriand took up the myth of the noble savage and brought it to its tragic culmination. It was in conformity with a long tradition in the history of ideas that European explorers and discoverers had dreamed "the American dream" of a paradise in the West inhabited by men who were good, free, and happy, living in a state of nature. The Jesuit missionaries of New France had contributed to the theory of the "bon" or "noble" savage. In fact, Jean-Jacques Rousseau's *Second Discourse on Inequality* (1755)—Chateaubriand was a disciple of Rousseau—was the philosophical climax of a centuries-old current of exoticism illustrated by many literary works.

Chateaubriand stated in his preface that he had enlarged upon the particular action and invited the reader "to see what fiction added to reality." It was by a process of adapting the facts, and most of all by poetic transformation into symbols that Chateaubriand, "the Enchanter," created *The Natchez*, his tragic romance, in prose. The opening lines, in the elegiac mode, suggest its two centers of interest: "In the shade of the American forest I will sing songs of solitude such as no mortal ears have yet heard; I will tell of your tragic fate, oh Natchez, oh nation of Louisiana, of whom only memories remain." On the one hand, the solitary and unhappy René, representing civilized man; on the other, the Indians of the doomed Natchez tribe: it will be an ill-fated encounter.

In the Chactas cycle the figure of the noble savage, a Natchez even though his name is the French name for Choctaw, is the character who binds *Atala*, *René*, and *The Natchez* together. Chactas is the narrator of *Atala*, in which he tells René the tale of his youth and tragic love for Atala, the Floridian half-breed, promised to virginity by her mother, and he is the listener in *René*, in which the Frenchman René tells him of his past and the love of his sister that will prevent him from ever finding happiness. Thus *Atala* and *René* stand detached from *The Natchez*, because they relate the heroes' pasts.

The plot of *The Natchez* can be summed up quickly: René, the melancholy young Frenchman, goes to Natchez to live with the Natchez tribe. He is adopted by Chactas as his son, is befriended by Outougamiz, and married to Outougamiz' sister Celuta. As events develop, the Natchez conspiracy is concocted by Ondouré to take revenge on René; although René is not a conspirator, he is suspected by the Indians, who are incited by his enemy Ondouré, and by the French, who believe he has betrayed them. Celuta and Outougamiz, meanwhile, are torn between love of René and love of their nation. All the characters perish at the time of the massacre or soon after. Chactas dies of old age, René is killed by Ondouré as the massacre begins and Outougamiz, Celuta, and Mila (Outougamiz's wife and René's friend) commit suicide when René is gone and they are among the Chicasaws.

The setting of the book is Natchez itself: the Indian huts grouped around Fort Rosalie and the banks of the Mississippi as far south as New Orleans and northward indefinitely. What Chateaubriand had asserted about *Atala* is also true of *The Natchez:* "I affirm that American wildlife is depicted in it with the most scrupulous accuracy."[17] This descriptive passage on the first page is obviously inspired by Charlevoix:

René, accompanied by his guide, had come up the Mississippi; his boat floated at the foot of the three bluffs that form a curtain concealing the lovely country of the children of the Sun. He jumped on to the bank, climbed up the steep slope, and reached the highest point of the three bluffs. The main village of the Natchez could be seen at some distance in a prairie dotted with groves of sassafras trees; Indian girls wandered here and there, as light as the deer they gamboled with; baskets suspended from long pieces of birch bark over their left arms, they were picking strawberries whose red juice stained their fingers and the grass around them.

But it is also obvious that Chateaubriand's poetic imagination has transformed the scene by dramatizing it (René is both spectator and actor);

and the idyllic tableau is already made ominous by the detail of the red juice, which foreshadows blood. In *The Natchez*, a very dramatic work, there are few of Chateaubriand's celebrated long descriptions like this one, but the text abounds with details of southern fauna and flora, not in catalogs, but often with effects of landscaping. Magnolias recur often, and the high dark masses of the magnolia treetops signal the village of Natchez. René swims in the river while the perfume of sweetgum and sassafras waft over the water. The calling of the mockingbird, the sighing of the painted bunting, and the buzzing of the hummingbird make up a wild symphony of the southern forest. However, while Chateaubriand's exoticism is authentically North American, even southern, some geographical impossibilities betray either Chateaubriand's ignorance or his original plans for a Canadian epic. Some examples are the gorgeous scene of the harvesting of wild rice, the impressive Indian council on the shores of Lake Superior, apparently only a few leagues from Natchez, and the charming custom Chateaubriand's Natchez Indians have of drinking maple syrup out of gourds. But these transplantations must be allowed and even welcomed as poetic license, for they are part of the strange beauty of the writer's imaginary Natchez. Fantasy is acceptable in the creation of a paradise soon to be lost.

The external action in the romance is the same as the events at Natchez in the 1720s, but as if enlarged by the magnifying glass of the poet's imagination. Time, like geography, is rather imprecise. René is supposed to arrive at Natchez in 1725, and the massacre occurs in 1727 (instead of 1729); one gigantic battle occurs between these two dates. Thus for dramatic effect Chateaubriand has condensed events that covered a longer period into the last years of peace before the disaster. *The Natchez* ends with the relation of the short, unhappy life of Celuta and René's daughter Amélie and a brief mention of the disappearance of the last of the Natchez scattered among the northern tribes. This corresponds chronologically to the account in the epilogue to *Atala* of Chateaubriand's meeting with Amélie and other Natchez survivors wandering in exile near Niagara, and so rounds off the time scheme, to bring the reader of Chateaubriand's day into contact with the last of the Natchez.

The epic poet adapts events by magnifying them. There is a kind of telescopic effect when *The Natchez* moves in the first books from the heavenly and hellish spheres where the actors are God, Satan, and the patron saints of France and New France, the moving spirits of the drama, down to earth where the drama will be played out. The greatest exaggerations are of the adversaries. Instead of the twenty-five men garrisoned at

Fort Rosalie, Chateaubriand advances no fewer than fifty companies of infantry, plus artillery, cavalry, assorted Swiss guards, and Canadian scouts, and displays them in a fantastic review on the plain above the river. The first battle reaches heights of horror, with the woods bespattered with the smoking brains and guts of the myriad warriors. For epic effect the Natchez conspiracy becomes a general revolution of *all* the tribes of the North American continent against the whites, after a speech made by the Natchez chief that rises to the dignity of the Declaration of Independence. One of the most memorable scenes in the book is the picturesque pageant of representatives from all the North American tribes to their council meeting.

But some Parisian critics sniffed disdainfully at the notion of writing an epic about a subject as limited as "the massacre of a few Frenchmen around a shanty." Perhaps the epic mode was already *démodé* by 1827. In fact, Chateaubriand eliminated supernatural elements and heroic allusions from the second part of *The Natchez*. The "appalling catastrophe" that ends the work (on the day of the massacre Celuta is raped by René's assassin, lying next to René's body, in his blood) belongs to another kind of *démesure* or disproportion, the frenzy of early romanticism. "All this is in the taste of the times when people only want scenes of upheaval that unsettle the soul," said Chateaubriand to a prospective editor.[18]

Indeed, it is the characters and their passions that take over the second part of *The Natchez* and that still interest the reader of today. Chateaubriand's Frenchmen and Indians are, of course, characters of *romance*; that is, they are types, each with a predominating trait that makes him or her larger than life. But heroes or villains are not all on one side; Chateaubriand gives his sympathy impartially to both French and Indians, because *The Natchez*, written during the French Revolution, began as an apology for liberty and was to be a paean to the Indians who attempted to throw off the tyranny of the whites. On the other hand, because the author was constrained to justify Christianity, he had to show the necessity of the evangelization of the savages. Thus, in the "supernatural" part, God is with the French, and it is Satan who inspires the Natchez with the idea of the conspiracy and the massacre instead of a declared war.

The two historical characters, Chépar, the commander of Fort Rosalie, and d'Artaguette, a young officer, are both fictionalized as brave soldiers. D'Artaguette always defends the Indians, and Chépar, no longer the unscrupulous, greedy trafficker depicted by Dumont and Le Page du

Pratz, is in Chateaubriand simply misguided and hoodwinked by the two-faced Febriano, Ondouré's agent, a kind of Iago in the drama. The solitary René was to become the type of the nineteenth-century romantic hero whose eternal ennui is the *mal du siècle*. René is alienated, ill-adapted in civilization or in a state of nature. There are some minor French characters, all friendly to the Indians.

How authentic are Chateaubriand's Natchez Indians? The writer borrowed heavily from Charlevoix in order to render tribal customs faithfully. But the real interest of the work lies in his having humanized the Natchez. Although individually each one represents a limited set of characteristics, as a group of characters they are unexpectedly complex. It is true that they are sentimentalized and shed a lot of eighteenth-century tears, but they are not all *bons sauvages*, although most of them are certainly "noble savages." Chateaubriand emphasizes their savagery and gives several examples of unrivaled ferocity: Ondouré, a truly sadistic devil devoured by lust, jealousy, and ambition, is the villain of the plot. In the sachem Adario, Chateaubriand depicts an equally ferocious savage who strangles his grandchild rather than allow him to become a slave; but this act rather supports the "liberty or death" theme and gives an example of Indian courage and inflexibility. Outougamiz also displays incredible bravery in his devotion to his friend René. The simplicity and candor of this man of action are opposed to René's civilized complexity and worldweariness. Chactas, the wise, blind sachem, is the real embodiment of the noble savage, resembling a sage of antiquity, as was traditional. "More than half civilized," after this trip to France, he becomes a vehicle for the author's commentary on French manners. He is like a combination of Cooper's brave Indian Chingachgook, and old Leatherstocking himself, representing the best in nature and civilization.

The women play an important role, as is appropriate in the Natchez tribe, where the monarchy was hereditary through the females. Here, too, there is a contrast between the violent and passionate Akansie, mother of the Sun, and the pure young heroines, Celuta and Mila. Chateaubriand's Indian women are very different from Cooper's genteel paleface heroines and really represent something new in literature. For the first time, an Indian "squaw" became subject rather than object. Much of the drama is focalized by Celuta, torn as she is between love of country and love of her foreign husband. In her, Chateaubriand delineates the anguish of the primitive woman trying to understand a civilized man.

And here we touch upon the main theme of *The Natchez*, which is the shock of cultures and races, the conflict between civilized and natural man, Old World and New. With an interesting subplot about the slaves' conspiracy, African joins American in confronting the European. One aspect of this theme is the nostalgia for the liberty of the savages before they were despoiled and enslaved by the whites. Of course it was paradoxical to choose the Natchez, who had the most despotic system of all the tribes, to represent liberty. Chateaubriand counters this problem in advance by showing a conflict within the tribe between Chactas and Adario, who had established a freer society, and the evil Ondouré, who wished to bring back the old system. But the real merit of *The Natchez* is in the problem of communication and comprehension between the two cultures. This problem is dramatized by Chactas, who is caught between two worlds; by René, who is alone and cannot find happiness with his Indian wife; and by Mila, who would save René but is condemned by her tribe. Friendship and love, the highest values in the book, attempt to bridge the gap, but love is often unrequited, and all the couples of friends and lovers are, at last, separated by death. René symbolizes the white man who dreams of a new life in the wilderness, but who can only be disillusioned. Ironically, he is the instrument of destruction of the savage way of life he admired, for as their revolt turns against them, the doomed Natchez announce the vanishing of the American Indian.

Chateaubriand's *The Natchez*, then, is more than a re-creation of a lost world, it is the tragedy of a failed utopian harmony of the races in "this charming country that could be called a second paradise."[19]

Notes

1. François-René de Chateaubriand, *Les Natchez* in *Oeuvres romanesques et voyages*, ed. Maurice Regard, Bibliothèque de la Pléiade (Paris: Gallimard, 1969).

2. François-René de Chateaubriand, *Mémoires d'outre-tombe*, 1, 307, quoted in Gilbert Chinard, *L'Exotisme américain dans l'oeuvre de Chateaubriand* (Paris: Librairie Hachette et Cie., 1918), 24.

3. See J. Pommier, "Chateaubriand en Amérique: le Cycle de Chactas" in *Dialogues avec le Passé* (Paris: Nizet, 1967).

4. Maurice Regard, Introduction, *Le Voyage en Amérique* in *Oeuvres romanesques et Voyages*, 600; Chateaubriand, *Essai sur les révolutions*, I, 29, quoted in Chinard, *L'Exotisme*, 69, 72.

5. Regard, Introduction, *Le Voyage en Amérique*, 60; Chinard, *L'Exotisme*, 86.

6. *Journal de d'Iberville*, Margry 4, 404–16, quoted in Pierre Heinrich, *La Louisiane sous la Compagnie des Indes 1717–1731*, Thèse, Paris, 1906 (Paris: Librairie Orientale et Américaine, n.d.), xxxiii; Richebourg G. McWilliams (ed. and trans.), *Fleur de Lys and Calumet: Being the Pénicaut Narrative of French Adventure in Louisiana* (Baton Rouge: Louisiana State University Press, 1953), 28, 83.

7. John Ray Skates, *Mississippi: A Bicentennial History* (New York: W. W. Norton, 1979), 27; Antoine de la Mothe Cadillac, Letters to Pontchartrain, February 20, March 1, May 10, 1714, Colonial Archives, C 13 III, 418–19, 465–66, 480, quoted in Heinrich, *La Louisiane*, lxviii.

8. Skates, *Mississippi*, 29.

9. Ibid.

10. Heinrich, *La Louisiane*, 229; Memoire du Conseiller d'Ausseville, January, 1732, Colonial Archives, C 13, XIV, folios 263–64; Abbé Le Mascrier, *Mémoires historiques sur la Louisiane composées sur les mémoires de M. Dumont* (2 vols.; Paris: Cl. J.B. Bauche, 1753), 125–28, quoted in Heinrich, *La Louisiane*, 231.

11. Le Page du Pratz, *Histoire de la Louisiane* (3 vols.; Paris: de Bure, 1758), 3, 244–50; and Le Mascrier, *Mémoires*, 2, 135–36; Letters from Périer to the "Controleur Général" and to Maurepas, March 18, April 10, 1730, Colonial Archives C 13 XII, folios 291–92, 301, in Heinrich, *La Louisiane*, 232.

12. James Adair, *History of the American Indians* (London, 1775), iii, 353, in Heinrich, *La Louisiane*, 234.

13. Letter from Diron d'Artaguette, February 9, 1730, Colonial Archives C 13 XII, folios 371–72; and Le Mascrier *Mémoires*, 144–45, 153, 155–59; Père de Charlevoix, *Histoire et description générale de la Nouvelle France* (6 vols.; Paris: Rolin Fils, Librairie, 1744), LV, 248, in Heinrich *La Louisiane*, 236, 237.

14. Le Page du Pratz, *Histoire*, 3, 241–53, 259; and Le Mascrier, *Mémoires*, 135–36 in Heinrich, *La Louisiane*, 237.

15. Le Page du Pratz, *Histoire*, 3, 289–90, 327.

16. Skates, *Mississippi*, 31.

17. Chateaubriand, Préface, *Atala*, 1805, 30.

18. *Revue encyclopédique*, 35, 1827, quoted in Regard "Accueil de la critique," 157; Chateaubriand, Letter of January 6, 1798, quoted in Regard, Introduction, *Les Natchez*, 15.

19. Dumont, "Poème en vers touchant l'établissement de la Louisiane connue sous le nom de Mississippi avec tout ce qui s'y est passé depuis 1716," Bibliothèque de l'Arsenal, Paris, 3459 (117 B.F.).

Some Sources of Pre-1830 Natchez History in Spanish Archives

ALFRED E. LEMMON

I. Natchez Under Spanish Rule, 1779–1798

John Francis Bannon, S.J., has observed that during the Spanish occupation of the Mississippi Valley relatively few Spaniards actually resided there. Documents reveal that top officials and their entourages, some soldiers, merchants, and clerics were Spanish, but just as only a few buildings in New Orleans—and none in the middle valley—date from the Spanish period, the majority of the population was not Spanish. Yet the Spaniards were not without lasting influence. They oriented the valley toward the Gulf of Mexico and the Caribbean, in contrast to the northern, Canadian orientation of the French.[1]

Natchez was under Spanish rule from 1779 through 1798. During the early years of the Spanish period, Natchez was governed by commandants, or military officers, who served, according to Jack D. L. Holmes, as "police captains, justices of the peace, consular officials, notaries public, sheriffs, judges, and military leaders," who in general strove to maintain law and order on the frontier. Eventually, the commandants were replaced by a governor of the Natchez District. The first, Manuel Gayoso de Lemos, arrived at his post in 1789. The governor of Natchez was subordinate to the governor general of Louisiana and West Florida, who, headquartered in New Orleans, was responsible to the captain general in Havana. All received orders from the secretary of war concerning military matters and from the Council of the Indies on other questions. Natchez, like New Orleans and other Spanish possessions in

43

the region, depended upon irregularly arriving subsidies from Mexico. The Code O'Reilly (1769) with origins in the *Recopilación de las Leyes de las Reynos de Indias* (1543) provided guidelines for the governance of the Natchez District.[2]

The district was the embodiment, par excellence, of frontier life. The less than ideally placed fort at Natchez, built on the site of the French Fort Rosalie, was vulnerable. A more important fort, Nogales, near the confluence of the Yazoo and Mississippi rivers, was a response to feared American expansionism. Even farther north, the fort at Chickasaw Bluffs (Memphis, Tennessee) was vital for the defense not only of Natchez, but of all of lower Louisiana. Members of the Louisiana Infantry formed a permanent military force in the Natchez region, yet at Natchez personnel remained a persistent weakness. The Natchez District was particularly vulnerable to Indian threats; officials engineered an uneasy truce by the constant reminder that Americans attracted to the region by the generous offers of the Spanish Crown were to be treated as subjects of that same crown. Eventually, in 1793, Indian and Spaniard formed an alliance, presumably to guard against United States expansion.[3]

The few products of the district—including tobacco, indigo, and cotton—met with varying degrees of success, and scarce manufactured goods sold at greatly inflated prices. The pleasures of life were necessarily simple, and gardening was a particular delight. Indeed, characteristic of frontier life, where economic survival itself was a major accomplishment, "signs of cultural, educational, and aesthetic interests" were noticeably absent. His Catholic Majesty attended to the spiritual welfare of his subjects by sending Irish priests trained at Salamanca, though a fair degree of ecumenical tolerance prevailed. With the Treaty of San Lorenzo in 1795, Spain permitted the navigation of the Mississippi River by the United States, as well as the right of deposit at New Orleans. On March 30, 1798, the Spanish flag was lowered at Natchez for the last time.[4]

As noted, the Spanish period was a time of change for the Natchez District. Under French and British rule, its isolation had produced a great deal of indifference from those in charge. Madrid, by contrast, sought to promote Natchez and lure American settlers. In order to do so, Spanish officials chose to adapt their official policies to the special and demanding circumstances of the hour.[5]

The historiography of Spanish Louisiana, which included Natchez, reflects the frontier environment and the Spanish defense, trade, and

Indian policies. Two basic bibliographical essays are Charles Edwards O'Neill, S.J., "The State of Studies in Spanish Colonial Louisiana," and Light Townsend Cummins, "Spanish Louisiana," in *A Guide to the History of Louisiana*. Cummins' more recent essay is a positive response to O'Neill's hope that studies in Spanish Louisiana would not proceed in "quick spurts" but rather in a continuing flow. Cummins stresses the increased number of important studies now available in the English language and views the post-World War II era as the setting for a "dramatic expansion in scholarly interest in Spanish Louisiana," a result of renewed accessibility to Spanish archives, the growth of microfilm, grant support, and ease of travel.[6] It is hoped, and to be expected, that the approaching quincentennial of the discovery of the New World will provide further stimulation of Spanish Louisiana studies.

II. Unity and Diversity:
A Sample of Some Spanish Archives

There are approximately 160 archival depositories in Spain with materials relevant to the New World. Excluded from this count are the numerous parish and notarial archives of every city and village containing information about individuals who migrated from the peninsula to the Americas; nor does it include the archives of the powerful companies that engaged in trans-Atlantic trade during the colonial period. Pre- or post-1830 Natchez documentation does not necessarily exist in these 160 depositories, which owe their existence to a variety of sources: the great noble families, religious institutions (both diocesan and religious orders), cultural institutions, government agencies, and the Spanish agency for archives and libraries. Natchez material is usually, but not exclusively, found within collections categorized as "Luisiana." The vast bulk of the Spanish documents relating to the Louisiana territory was returned to Spain, placing scholars of this region in a far more dependent position than researchers devoted to the rest of the Spanish New World.[7]

Spanish archivists and historians have been most conscious of their roles as guardians of documentation relevant to the overseas possessions of the Spanish empire. The *Real Academia de la Historia*, founded in 1738, was charged in 1755 with the responsibility of *Cronista Mayor de Indias*. Since its founding in 1751, the Academy's library has assembled a sizable collection of documents, acquired through purchase, exchange, and donations from members. With a strong publications history, the Academy is now publishing a series of catalogs of its various collections on the occasion of the five-hundredth anniversary of the

45

discovery of the New World.[8] Such activity, hardly unique, stands as a sign of the numerous avenues of research currently being opened to scholars.

The *archivo* of the *Ministerio do Asuntos Exteriores* (the Foreign Office) is divided into two sections. The "historic" section contains approximately 4,500 *legajos* or bundles of documents. The material in that section dates primarily from the eighteenth and nineteenth centuries. MS 213, a description of the Province of Louisiana dating from the late eighteenth century, is an example of relevant materials in that depository. Documents generated after 1900 are maintained in another division and are not usually available to the general public.[9]

Among military archives, the *Servicio Histórico Militar* in Madrid is an underemployed resource. Comprising a library of 500,000 volumes, and a cartographic section of 25,000 maps and plans, it has a large collection of manuscripts. These documents, in their numerous descriptions of forts along the Mississippi River, attest to Spain's preoccupation with defense of the region.[10] The *Archivo General Militar* in Segovia boasts approximately 68,000 *legajos* containing a large number of *hojas de servicios* (brief résumés of Spanish military personnel). The *Servicio Geográfico del Ejército* in Madrid, a relatively recent institution created in 1939, incorporates material from the *Déposito de la Guerra* (established in 1810). The archive of the *Museo Naval* in Madrid, established in 1843, incorporates material from the *Déposito Hidrográfico*, founded in 1789. It harbors extensive map collections and historical accounts and descriptions of the land and people. MS 133, "Padrón de latitudes y longitudes en las costas de la Luisiana y la Florida," is of interest to historical geographers since it inventories the Spanish posts of the Mississippi Valley and Gulf Coast in relation to Ellicott's line, Cadiz, Greenwich, and other relevant cities; Natchez' geographic position, for example, is given in relation to that of Philadelphia.

The *Biblioteca Nacional* in Madrid, noted for its collections of rare books, also has a superb manuscript collection. Natchez documentation ranges from accounts of inhabitants to information on the defense system of the post. The *Reglamiento General* of 1785 reveals there was to be one priest in Natchez, at the cost of 240 pesos per year. In periods of peace, there were to be an infantry captain with sixty soldiers, a hospital with a doctor, and a storehouse with a manager. All of these people and their supplies were to cost 6,000 pesos per year. Esteban Minor, righthand man to the commandants and governor before being appointed governor himself in 1797, was to receive 480 pesos per year.[11]

Esteban Miro, writing to Bernardo de Gálvez on November 7, 1782, urged that the fort at Natchez, in need of physical improvements and weapons, be revitalized. Miro stressed the importance of clarifying relations with Indians and cited examples of Indian relations with both the English and the Negroes.[12]

The section "Estado" of the *Archivo Histórico Nacional* in Madrid, in addition to the maps and plans listed in the appendix, contains information on the Aaron Burr conspiracy and his activities in the Natchez District during 1807, as well as information on expeditions by Americans from Natchez against Spaniards in Texas during 1818. The correspondence relative to Diego Morphy, Spanish vice-consul at Natchez, and later of New Orleans, comments upon living conditions in the district. Morphy twice states he could not exist in Natchez on the salary provided him, and petitions that his salary be made equal to that of consuls elsewhere in the United States during the early nineteenth century.[13]

The *Archivo General de Simancas*, near Valladolid, was designated as the depository for documents arriving from the Indies by Charles V in 1544. It fulfilled that mandate until the 1788 decree of Charles III ordered them transferred to the newly created *Archivo General de Indias* of Seville. During the uncertainties of the nineteenth century, Simancas suffered tremendously. Not until 1939, when General Francisco Franco took an interest in that archive, did improvements begin. After that date, new storage areas, photographic facilities, and a highly trained professional staff were developed. Famous as the depository of the monarchs of the "House of Austria," it is full of eighteenth-century material concerning the Americas.[14]

Although there is a wealth of Natchez material in this archive, there is space here to call attention only to two maps and plans. The copy of the "Representación de las barrancas de Margot o Chicasaw Bluffs sobre el Misisipi . . ." is accompanied by correspondence dated 1795 concerning the construction of Fort San Fernanco at the site.[15]

A plan for a Natchez prison, dating from 1792, is accompanied by an account of Fort Natchez, which again highlights the supremacy of Nogales, and argues the economic considerations for reducing Natchez in importance. The plan suggests Natchez as an appropriate place for a prison: a prison was important if the district was to be properly policed, and the size of the population demanded such a prison. Manuel Gayoso de Lemos submitted on June 14, 1792, an account of the population of the "Gobierno de Natchez." The population of 4,346 was divided by district, with an account of both men and women, according to age groups. [16] Although progress on proposals for the prison was apparently slow, because of the absence of properly trained engineers, Guillermo Dunbar prepared a relatively simple plan for the prison, which, officials deemed, should be of wood and really of little monetary value, a common practice in the Province of Louisiana.

An inventory of various fortifications along the Mississippi River reveals that of the ninety-four cannons designated for New Orleans, only fifty-one were present. In contrast, the smaller fort of Natchez, ninety leagues from New Orleans, had all 16 of its cannons. The report further notes that Natchez had been reduced to a primitive state with one officer and forty men. Fort Nogales, with twenty-eight cannons (none missing), was larger. One hundred-twenty leagues from New Orleans, it guarded the Mississippi River and was considered the "most advanced fort in Louisiana on the East Bank of the Mississippi." It was permanently fortified at a cost of 60,000 pesos per year. A 1795 report suggested that Natchez should be considered the first priority. Other documents reveal that frequent rains had weakened Fort Natchez and that some questioned even the advisability of repairs. [17]

And though these depositories contain a variety and wealth of information about the Natchez District, it is unfortunate that one particular archive does not appear to do so. The archive of the Royal Botanical Garden, situated adjacent to the Prado Museum, contains numerous records of the various scientific expeditions of the eighteenth century. Regretfully, none appear to have visited any part of the "Provincia de la Luisiana." [18]

United by their guardianship of materials for the history of the Americas, diverse in that their holdings result from the parent institutions' purposes, some of these archives are less frequently used than their holdings warrant. It is, nonetheless, important to remember that these are but a few references to the archives, designed to whet the appetite. Furthermore, there may well be material in archives not noted here.

III. Archive of an Overseas Empire:
The Archivo General de Indias

The *Archivo General de Indias* is the only archive in Spain dedicated exclusively to the care of documents from the Spanish Americas and Philippines. The documents housed there were generated primarily by the Spanish administrative agencies concerned with the New World and the Far East. Both agencies, *La Casa de Contratación* and *El Real y*

Supremo Consujo de Indias, date from the early sixteenth century. The *Casa de Contratación* (House of Trade) licensed and supervised all ships, merchants, passengers, goods, crews, and equipment passing to and from the Indies. The *Consjo de Indias* (Council of the Indies) exercised supreme governmental and judicial power over the Spanish American colonies; it prepared and dispatched all laws and decrees relating to the administration, taxation, and policies of the American dominions with the approval, and in the name, of the king. No important plan of action by a local government could be undertaken without its approval. It served, also, as the court of last resort.[19]

In the late eighteenth century, at the suggestion of historian Juan Bautista Muñoz (1745–ca. 1799), officials decided to gather and place in one archive all documents resulting from the diverse activities of these two agencies, and on October 11, 1778, generated the first written proposal to create this archive. In 1784 Muñoz drew up a plan for the archive and designated the materials it was to collect. In 1785 the impressive building in which it is located was remodeled, and in the same year, the documents began to arrive. After two hundred years of service to the international scholarly community, the Archive of the Indies remains an inexhaustible primary resource for historians of Spanish America.[20]

Louisiana and, accordingly, Natchez material is found primarily, but not exclusively, in two sets of papers—the Santo Domingo papers and the Cuban papers. The names of these collections are derived from their provenance. As late as the eighteenth century, the jurisdictional area of the Captaincy General (an area less important, but critical, due to foreign aggression or Indian problems) and Audiencia (the chief organ of royal authority) of Santo Domingo comprised all the islands of the West Indies and Venezuela. Although only nominally belonging to Santo Domingo, Florida was always so regarded in the organization schemes of the Spanish archives; after its cession from France, Louisiana was briefly placed in the same special category as Florida. The 1768 insurrection, however, led to its inclusion, for judicial reasons, in the Captaincy General of Havana and in the Audiencia of Santo Domingo. After 1795 it was responsible to the Audiencia at Havana.[21]

The wide variety of Louisiana documentation available in the Santo Domingo papers is a result of the province's judicial relation with that Audiencia. The specific legajos relevant to Louisiana, numbered 2528 to 2689, cover the years 1762 to 1810. These 148 legajos contain material pertinent to the study of such varied topics as native tribes (their customs and reactions to the French, Spanish, and American governments), migration to the colony, and natural disasters. Students of social, political, economic, and military history will find an abundance of material. Indeed, scholars interested in the greater Mississippi River Valley and Gulf Coast will find important documents here, as will students of other regions of the United States. For example, there is information on Charleston, Boston, and Philadelphia, as well as on New Jersey, New York, North and South Carolina, and Virginia. Among countries represented in the Santo Domingo papers are Argentina, Cuba, England, Holland, Ireland, Mexico, Spain, and Santo Domingo.[22]

The Santo Domingo papers are also important in that they represent a milestone in the historiography of the region and of Spain. In 1958 Loyola University in New Orleans proposed to undertake a project for Louisiana documentation in Spain similar to the Vatican microfilm project of St. Louis University; Spanish policy at that time, however, did not permit the microfilming of an entire *legajo*. The granting of permission for the project, which required entire *legajos* to be microfilmed, represented a major change in Spanish archival practice. Since permission for that project was given in 1960, other regions throughout the world have begun similar projects. It stands as a striking example of how a relatively small institution, in this case a university, took an idea, implemented it, and changed the course of historiography.[23]

While the format of reproducing the documents of microfilm was new, the idea of reproducing the documents for use by both government officials and scholars was not new. The Spanish Crown itself engaged scholars and scribes to assemble and copy vast quantities of documents scattered in distant archives, as did religious orders such as the Jesuits. Indeed, the state of Mississippi commissioned the copying by hand of documents in the Archive of the Indies during the first decade of the twentieth century.[24]

The themes of defense, trade, and Indian policy permeate Natchez documents in the Santo Domingo papers. Documents such as the 1786 instructions given Philipe Treviño, commandant of Natchez, and suggestions for restructuring the defense systems and Forts Natchez and Nogales likewise reflect Spanish policies in the region. The analysis of supplies of Fort Nogales in 1794 provides concrete information on military preparedness. The account of government affairs for one year beginning in 1791 reflects the detail of documentation available: the amount of information, for example, about the responsibilities and remuneration of such individuals as interpreter Francisco St. Jermain, officials Manuel Gayoso de Lemos and Carlos Gran Pré, and of *Secretaria* José Vidal, stands as testimony to the detail with which Spanish life in the valley can be reconstructed from extant documents. Martín Navarro's *informe* to José de Gálvez, for another example, noted that the Natchez District deserved more attention regarding the cultivation of tobacco. The high elevation and fertile soil, he claimed, produced a superior crop. Navarro's report sheds light on the socioeconomic structure of the district in its report that there were only two classes of people, the comfortable and the very poor: the resulting differences in lifestyle between the two classes are attested to in all aspects of life, as seen in how they differed in the production of tobacco.[25]

The Cuban papers derive their name from the fact that for a considerable portion of the nineteenth century they formed part of the *Archivo General de Cuba* in Havana; they were moved to the Archive of the Indies between 1888 and 1889. The Louisiana documents had been subject to several moves beginning in 1804. In 1804 the Spanish commissioners for the transfer of Louisiana requested the various posts to classify and inventory all documents in their possession. Items relating to property, wills, marriages, and other personal interests were to be transferred to the French and then to the United States.[26] In turn, the documents were moved to Pensacola between 1804 and 1806. However, papers of the Treasure and Customs House were sent directly to Havana. In 1808 it was deemed more appropriate that the documents in Pensacola should be in Havana. Unfortunately, before that transfer of a major portion of documents in 1818 and 1819, fire destroyed many of the papers. During 1856 and 1857, the remaining documents were placed in their final order, basically according to topography.[27]

The Cuban papers relevant to Louisiana cover the period 1761 to 1821. The various subjects include politics (both internal and external); relations with the United States; Indian affairs; financial, military, social, and religious matters; and immigration. Employee records for Fort Nogales for 1791–1792 and 1794–1797, and Fort Natchez for 1781–1782, 1787–1789, 1791–1793, 1797, and 1802 contain information bearing upon all aspects of Spanish life. The *Guarda Almacen* (warehouse) records for 1794, 1795, and 1797 contain information necessary to an understanding of health care, defense, and Indian affairs. The accounting of 1793 of the Natchez warehouse is practically an inventory of items needed for survival on the frontier. Indian relations are attested to in the list of gifts and supplies given the Indians during the period 1781–1792. His Majesty's concern for the spiritual welfare of this remote, distant dominion is recorded in *legajos* 594 and 601, which concern the Irish priests sent to Natchez and certain church ornaments, respectively. One of the *legajos* important for Natchez history was misplaced and is found not with "Luisiana" documents, but with those of "Costa Firme."[28]

Fortunately, scholars currently concerned with the history of Spanish Natchez have a distinct advantage. Given current conditions, it is unlikely they will experience a fate similar to the American diplomat and literary figure Washington Irving, who spent one entire year (1828–1829) primarily waiting for access to the Archive of the Indies to prepare revisions needed for the second edition of his work on Columbus.[29] By the thorough, systematic exploration of the Spanish archives, information can be retrieved that will provide a detailed account of Natchez under Spanish rule.

APPENDIX

Natchez and the Natchez District:
Selected Maps and Plans in Spanish archives

The maps and plans listed are all manuscript items. Although printed ones exist in these archives, they are omitted for present purposes. Items are arranged according to depository. The descriptions are based upon those used in the archives; the reference number provided is that employed by the archive. In cases where the descriptions are based upon a printed catalog, appropriate reference is given; in other instances they are based on the card catalog. Dates are given in parentheses, reference numbers in brackets. As the descriptions remain in the original Spanish, brief English titles are given in quotation marks. The Historic New Orleans Collection (THNOC) has a microfilm copy of the maps and plans available for study.

Archivo General de Indias[30]

[95]	Plano figurativo de la tierra del nombrado Juan Rauls . . . en el distrito del fuerte panmure de Natches. (1783) "Plan of the land of Juan Rauls in Fort Panmure of the Natchez District."
[136]	Apunte para un plano ¿del hospital de Natchez? (1790) "Note for a hospital in Natchez?"
[138]	Mapa de los terrenos de las compañías de Virginia y de la Carolina del Sur en el Yasu, entre el Mississippi, Natchez, Río de la Mobila y río Tenese. (1791) "Map showing the lands of the Virginia Company and South Carolina, between the Mississippi River, Natchez and Tennessee and Mobile Rivers."
[140]	Fuerte de los Nogales, proyectado y delineado por el coronel don Manuel Gayoso y Lemos, gobernador de la plaza y distrito de Natchez. (1791) "Fort Nogales, as planned by Manuel Gayoso de Lemos."
[157]	Plano de unas tierras próximas a Natchez. (1794) "Plan of some land near Natchez."
[180]	Mapa de la parte del Mississippi situada al sur de la confluencia del Rouge y Chajalaya, con proyecto de cortar un lazo para breviar la navegacion entre Natchez y Nueva Orleans. (1796) "Map of part of the Mississippi River, with a proposed route to abbreviate the distance between Natchez and New Orleans."
[183]	Perfil del revestimiento del Mont Vigio hasta su foso en Nogales. (1797) "Profile of the revetment 'Mont Vigio' as far as the foss at Nogales."

[189]   Dos perfils de parapetos. "Estado de las fortificaciones del puesto de los Nogales en primeros de agosto de 1797 y de sus edificios militares." (1789) "Two elevations of parapets at Fort Nogales."

Archivo General de Simancas[31]

M.P. y D.   XIX-45 Copia de la "Representación de las barrancas de Margot of Chicasaw Bluffs sobre el Misisipi. . . ." (1795) "Copy of Margot or Chicasaw Bluffs. . . ."

M.P. y D.   XIX-69 Plano del reducto de los Nogales. (1791) "Plan of Nugales."

M.P. y D.   XIX-131 Plano de una cárcel para la plaza de Natchez. (1792) "Plan for the proposed prison at Natchez."

Archivo Histórico Nacional[32]

[305]   Estados Unidos, región sur-oriental. Al dorso "Luisiana y Florida." (1760) "United States, southeastern region, Louisiana and Florida."

[306]   Estados Unidos, región sur-oriental. (1760) "United States, southeastern region."

[310]   Estados Unidos, región sur-oriental. Se indican las tierras de los cherakees y los límites convenidos con Estados Unidos e Inglaterra. (1793) "United States, southeastern region. Cherakee territory and boundaries between the United States and England are indicated."

[311]   Plano topográfico copiado de varios ingleses que comprehenden los estableimientos americanos al occidente do los Montes Apalaches, cuyos ríos desaguan en el Ohio y sucesivamente en el Misisipy. (1787) "Topographical map copied from various English maps, illustration of the American establishments west of the Apalachans, whose rivers flow into the Ohio and Mississippi rivers."

[312]   Confederación de las tribus indias de los Montes Apalaches, ríos Ohio y Mississippi, ataque de Cumberland por los Cheraquis y Creek." (c. 1792) "Indian tribes of the Apalachan mountains and Mississippi and Ohio rivers. . . ."

[335]   Provincia de la Luisiana poseida de la nación francesa. . . . (1718) "Province of Louisiana in possession of the French."

[336]   Sobre el mapa hay algunos datos acerca del terreno, como montes ricos en planta; ríos abundantes de peces; dias de

54

navegación. "Indicated on the map is information about plant life on various mountains, fish in rivers, and days required for navigation."

[340]   Representación de las barrancas de Margot o Chicasaw Bluffs sobre el Misisipi, cuyas barrancas la nación chicacha cede a la nación española. . . . (1795) "Margot or Chicasaw Bluffs on the Mississippi, that were ceded by the Chicachas to Spain."

[347]   Mapa de la parte septentrional de la provincia de Tejas y sus inmediaciones con la Luziana y Florida. (1769) "Map of the northern portions of the province of Texas and its environs of Louisiana and Florida."

[350]   Copia de el mapa que en 18 de diziembre de 1717 presentó don Juan de Olivan Rebolledo, oydor de la Real Audiencia de Mexico con su ynforme a el virrey de la Nueva España a consecuencia de el reconocimiento que hizo de extas provincias de orden de S. Exc. Comprende parte de Mejico, Tejas, y algo de la costa de Luisiana y Florida. "Copy of Juan de Olivan Rebolledo's map presented in 1717 to the Viceroy of New Spain. Resulting from his inspections of the region, it includes parts of Louisiana and Florida."

Biblioteca Nacional

[R327]   Carte du cours du Fleuve St. Louis depuis les Natchez, jusqui a son embouchure. (1743) "Map of the St. Louis River from Natchez to the mouth."

Ministerio do Asuntos Exteriores: Archivo Histórico.

[MS 213]   Descripción, de algunas provincias de la América Septentrional, con varios reflexiones politicas y militares. [c. 1790–1800] "Description of some provinces of North America, with various political and military reflections." Includes two maps.

Museo Naval

[VI-A-6]   Carte de la Louisiane dressée d'aprés les plans et memoires de ingenieurs quiont eté a la Louisiane. "Map of Louisiana based on plans and memoirs of engineers that served in Louisiana."

Servicio Geográfico Militar[33]

SECCIÓN: ESTADOS UNIDOS Y CANADA: LUISIANA.

[84]   Curso del Misisipi desde Nueva Orleans hacia el Norte. "Course of the Mississippi from New Orleans north."

[85]   Carte de la Louisiane et particulierement du fleuve Mississippi. "Map of Louisiana and in particular the Mississippi River."

Servicio Histórico Militar[34]

[D-9-18 (7259)]   Plano de la situación del Fuerte de Nogales en el río Mississippi. "Plan showing Fort Nogales on the Mississippi."

[D-10-37 (5058)]   Mapa de la parte de la Luisiana correspondiente a los limites en cuestion con los angloamericanos (1817). "Map of that portion of Louisiana whose boundary is in question with the United States."

Notes

1. Charles J. Fleener, "John Francis Bannon, S.J. (1905–86)," *Hispanic American Historical Review*, 67 (February, 1987), 139–42; John Francis Bannon, S.J., "The Spaniards in the Mississippi Valley: An Introduction," in John Francis McDermott (ed.), *The Spanish in the Mississippi Valley, 1762–1804* (Urbana: University of Illinois Press, 1964), 12.

2. Jack D. L. Holmes, "A Spanish Province, 1779–1798," in Richard Aubrey McLemore (ed.), *A History of Mississippi* (Hattiesburg: University and College Press of Mississippi, 1973), I, 159–60. This is perhaps the best concise history of Spanish Natchez.

3. *Ibid.*, 162, 165.

4. D. Clayton James, *Antebellum Natchez* (Baton Rouge: Louisiana State University Press, 1968), 37; Holmes, "Province," 167, 170, 171–73.

5. James, *Natchez*, 52–53.

6. Bannon, "Spaniards," in McDermott (ed.), *Valley*, 13, 16–25; Light Townsend Cummins, in "Spanish Louisiana," Light T. Cummins and Glenn Jeansonne (eds.), *A Guide to the History of Louisiana* (Westport, Conn.: Greenwood Press, 1982), 18–25; O'Neill, "State," 25.

7. Based on archives supplying information to the *Guía de Fuentes para la Historia de Ibero-América conservada en España* (Madrid: Dirección General de Archivos y Bibliotecas, 1966), hereinafter cited as *Guía*; José de la Peña y Camara, Ernest J. Burrus, S.J., Charles Edwards O'Neill, S.J., and Maria Teresa García Fernández, (eds.), *Catálogo de Documentos del Archivo General de Indias, Sección V, Gobierno, Audiencia de Santo Domingo sobre la Epoca Española de Luisiana* (Madrid and New Orleans: Dirección General de Archivos y Bibliotecas and Loyola University, 1968), xv.

8. *Guía*, II, 368–408; Alfred E. Lemmon, "The *Real Academia de la Historia* of Spain and the Celebration of the Anniversary of the Discovery of the Americas," *The Americas: A Quarterly Review*, 42 (1986), 347–49.

9. *Guía*, I, 187–90. Also consult: *Los Manuscritos del Archivo General y Biblioteca de*

Ministerio de Asuntos Exteriores (Madrid: Ministero de Asuntos Exteriores, 1974), 334–35.

10. *Guía,* I, 453–82, 485–86, 490–502. Consult Eric Beerman, "A Checklist of Louisiana Documents in the Servicio Histórico Militar in Madrid," *Louisiana History,* 20 (1979), 17–19. THNOC has a microfilm copy of selected documents from the Servicio Histórico Militar. Classification: 5.1.10.7, dated 1824.

11. *Guía,* II, 180–361. Also consult Julian Paz, *Catálogo de Manuscritos de América existentes en la Biblioteca Nacional* (Madrid: Tip. de Archives, 1933). "Reglamiento General de Empleados y sus obligaciones en la Provincia de la Luisiana," August 18, 1785. In "Colección de Documentos sobre la Luisiana, 1767–1792," 2, folio 62. Microfilm copy available at THNOC.

12. "Oficio de D. Esteban Miro a D. Bernardo Gálvez sobre su expedicion a Natchez y defensas que hizo en aquel fuerte, Nueva Orleans," November 7, 1782; Item 275 in Paz, *Catálogo.*

13. *Guía,* I, 3–26. A highly useful index is the multivolume *Documentos relativos a la Independencia de Norteamérica existentes en Archivos Españoles* (Madrid: Ministerio de Asuntos Exteriores, 1976). Archives included in the guide are: Archivo General de Indias, Archivo Histórico Nacional and the Archivo General de Simancas. Papeles de Estado, Legajo 5633. "Correspondencia de Don Carlos Martínez de Irujo, Ministro Plenipotenciario de España en los Estados Unidos con Don Pedro Cevallos, Secretaria de Estado." Letters 805, 807, and 813, and "Correspondencia de Don Valentín Foronda, Consul General, con Pedro Cevallos, Secretario de Estado," Letter 242; ibid., Legajo 5645, "Correspondencia de Don Mateo de la Serna," Expedientes #35 and #43; Legajo 5644, expediente #175. "Correspondencia de Don Luis de Onis."

14. Angel de la Plaza, *Guía del Investigador* (Madrid: Dirección General de Archivos y Bibliotecas, 1962), ix–xvii; *Guía del Archivo General de Simancas* (Madrid: Dirección General de Archivos y Bibliotecas, 1958), 5–14, I, 62–79.

15. Guerra Moderna, Legajo 7244, letters of September 17, 23, and 28 of 1795.

16. *Ibid.,* Legajo 6928, No. 232 (November 8, 1792) and "Estado que manifiesta la Población del Gobierno de Natchez." Microfilm copies of these items available at THNOC.

17. *Ibid.,* Legajo 7274, "Extracto del expediente No. 412 que manifiesta el estado de las Playas, Fuertas y Provincia de la Luisiana."

18. *Guía,* II, 440–44. During a visit in 1984, the author had the opportunity to meet with archivists and examine the holdings. On that basis this particular conclusion was reached.

19. José María de la Peña y Camara, *Archivo General de Indias de Sevilla: Guía del Visitante* (Madrid: Dirección General de Archivos y Bibliotecas, 1958), 67–70.

20. *Ibid.,* 53–64.

21. William Shepherd, *Guide to the Materials for the United States Archives (Simancas, the Archivo Historico Nacional, and Seville)* (Washington, D.C.: Carnegie Institution, 1907).

22. Peña y Camara, *Catálogo,* xv.

23. Charles Edwards O'Neill, S.J., "Recollections of the *Archivo General de Indias*" in *El Archivo General de Indias en mi Recuerdo* (Seville: Consejería de Cultura, 1985), 121–28. Microfilm copies of the Santo Domingo papers are at Loyola University at New

Orleans, Louisiana State University at Baton Rouge, The Historic New Orleans Collection, and the University of Southwestern Louisiana at Lafayette.

24. A splendid example is the career of José Antonio Pichardo (1748–1812), who in 1808 was commissioned by the viceroy of New Spain to assemble documentation on the question of boundaries between Louisiana and Texas. He collected 4,000 folios on the topic. The first volume was published as *Pichardo's Treatise on the Limits of Louisiana and Texas* (Austin: University of Texas, 1931–46), ed. Charles Wilson Hackett. In 1898 two young Mexican Jesuits were sent to the Jesuit archives in Loyola, Spain, to copy the references to the Mexican province in the "Diario de la expulsión del P. Mariano Luengo," a noted chronicler of the 1767 Jesuit expulsos. A copy of the work of the two young Mexicans is preserved in the Archive of the Mexican Province of the Society of Jesus. Dunbar Rowland, *Fifth Annual Report of the Director of the Department of Archives and History of the State of Mississippi, October 1, 1905–October 1, 1906*. (Nashville: Press of the Brandon Print Co., 1907). Bell and Howell Microfilm Company has produced a microfilm edition of the material, which is now located in that agency. Mississippi material in the French National Archives and the British Public Record Office were also copied during this period.

25. Santo Domingo, Legajo 2550, "Ynstrucción para el Comandante de Natchez, Don Phelipe Treviño," June 16, 1786; Legajo 2614, "Juan Ventura Morales to Pedro Varela y Ulloa," expediente #11; Legajo 2550, "Estado General de la Artileria, Montares, Pertrechos y demas efectos de la Provincia de la Luisiana por fin de diciembre de 1794"; Legajo 2560, "Estado que manifiesta el gobierno de Natchez, Luis de las Casas al Conde de Campo Alange" (#232); Legajo 2550, "Reglamiento general de Empleados," March 20, 1785; Legajo 2539, "Manuel Gayoso de Lemos, Titulo, Gobernador de la Plaza y Puesto de Natchez en el Distrio de la Provincia de Luisiana," February 7, 1789; Legajo 2539, "Don Carlos Grand Pré, Titulo, Gobernador del Fuerte y Distrito de Natchez en la Provincia de la Luisiana," December 12, 1796; Legajo 2539, "Don José Vidal, Nombramiento, Secretario del Gobierno del Fuerte de Natchez en Luisiana," December 26, 1792; Legajo 2633, September 12, 1782. For a detailed study consult: Brian E. Coutts, "Boom and Bust: The Rise and Fall of the Tobacco Industry in Spanish Louisiana, 1770–1790," *The Americas: A Quarterly Review*, 42 (1986), 289–309.

26. Although land records appear to be scarce in Spanish archives, the Historic New Orleans Collection has the following collections with information relevant to the Natchez District and land tenure: Louisiana Land Surveys (1787–1827), being a collection of over 1,000 surveyors' drawings, certificates, and notes. Natchez material is found in the following series: Alpha-Numerical (1786–1802); Natchez-Bouligny (1786–98); Natchez-Canonge (1787–97); Natchez-Pedesclaux (1789–93); Natchez-Undocketed (1787–1801); Natchez-Bound Volume (1787–97); Various Surveys (1788–1802).

The names of the various series for documents are derived from their organization, their region surveyor, or their physical condition. Material is indexed according to date, location, surveyor, and landowner (both grantees and adjacent landowners). MSS 79. Spanish Colonial Land Grant papers (1767–1834) is a small, artificial collection with information on the Natchez District. In addition, THNOC has a microfilm of material from the Clements Library of the University of Michigan. Spanish land grants from Louisiana are found in a variety of depositories throughout the United States, including: Tulane University, New Orleans Public Library, Clements Library (University of Michigan), Beinecke (Yale University), Louisiana State University, Louisiana State Archives and Records Service, and the Louisiana State Land Office.

27. The basic guide to North American documentation in the Cuban Papers is Roscoe R. Hill, *Descriptive Catalogue of the Documents Relating to the History of the United States in the Papeles Procedentes de Cuba Deposited in the Archivo General de Indias at Seville* (Washington, D.C.: Carnegie Institution, 1916), xii–xxvii. As outlined in O'Neill, "Recollections," a second microfilm project devoted to the Cuban Papers was begun by Loyola University and is being continued by the Historic New Orleans Collection and Louisiana State University, Baton Rouge. To date, the following *legajos* have been filmed and are available at Loyola University, Louisiana State University, and the Historic New Orleans Collection, legajos 488–560 and 562–630. Louisiana State University and the Historic New Orleans Collection also have 181–227B. The following have been prepared for filming and are currently being microfilmed: 1–100; 631–706; 772; 830; 2317A and B; 2318–21. The following have been prepared and are awaiting microfilming: 103–80; 1045–47; 1232–33; 1393–94; 1425; 1440; 1446; 1525–26; 1533; 2351; 2336–37; 2357–72.

28. Cuban Papers 538A, "Natchez, Asientos de los Empleados de dicho Puerto," and "Nogales: Asientos de los Empleados de dicho Puesto"; Cuban Papers, legajo 524. Comprobantes de Guarda Almacen de Natchez, 1794–95 Ramo de artilleria; ramo de indios, ramo de hospital, ramo de fortificaciones y víveres. Legajo 523A, Comprobantes del Guarda Almacen de Natchez, 1797. Ramo de víveres, ramo de hospital, ramo de fortificaciones y víveres. Legajo 522, Ramo de fortifacaciónes y víveres. Cuentaordenada de Guarda Almacen don Francisco Candel, pertencientes del Puesto de Natchez del año de 1793. Legajo 536 contains accounts and vouchers of the *guardas almacenes* for the *Ramo de Indios* for 1782–1792. Consult Jack D. L. Holmes, "Irish Priests in Spanish Natchez," *Journal of Mississippi History*, 29 (1976), 169–80. Fully one-half the documents, including various *relaciones* and *estados* are useless due to water damage. Account vouchers of Francisco Candel, *Guarda Almacen* of Natchez, for 1795, survive in relatively good condition.

29. Eric Beerman, "Washington Irving en el Archivo General de Indias (1828/1829)," *Archivo Hispalensis*, 68 (1985), 153–65.

30. Julio González, *Catálogo de Mapas y Planos de la Florida y la Luisiana* (Madrid: Dirección General del Patrimonio Artístico, Archivos, y Múseos, 1979).

31. María Concepción Alvárez Terán, *Mapas, Planos y Dibujos [Años 1503–1805]* (Valladolid: Dirección General de Bellas Artes, Archivos, y Bibliotecas, 1980).

32. Pilar León Tello, *Mapas, Planos y Dibujos de la Sección de Estado del Archivo Histórico Nacional* (Madrid: Ministerio de Cultura, 1979).

33. *Cartoteca Histórica: Indice de Mapas y Planos Historicos de America* (Madrid: Servicio Geográfico del Ejercito, 1974).

34. *Catálogo General de la Cartoteca* (Madrid: Servicio Histórico Militar, 1981).

The Natchez Trace Collection

Don E. Carleton

Spanning the era between the late 1770s and early 1900s, the Natchez Trace Collection at the University of Texas at Austin comprises a treasure of original manuscripts, financial and legal records of every type, maps, sheet music, newspapers, pamphlets, ephemera, photographs, diaries, and other archival documents of various description. Its contents reflect the lives and activities of government officials, politicans, soldiers, bankers, farmers, jurists, planters, merchants, attorneys, physicians, clergy, educators, slaves, and homemakers who lived and worked in the parishes and counties of Louisiana and Mississippi, particularly in the Natchez region.

The collection gets its name from the fact that an important component documents the historical development of that region in Mississippi traversed by the old Indian trail and road linking Nashville with Natchez. As a cohesive whole, however, the entire collection also documents important aspects of the history of much of the lower Mississippi River Valley.

Carefully pieced together by a private collector during the early decades of the twentieth century, the Natchez Trace Collection remained untapped by scholarly researchers after it was assembled over fifty years ago, until the University of Texas at Austin acquired it in December, 1985. It is now housed at the university's Eugene C. Barker Texas History Center.

Because of its size—well over 450 linear feet—and complexity the Natchez Trace Collection awaits years of careful investigation by researchers before the details of its contents can be known. Its general components, however, are already clear. There are, for example, well over one hundred individual collections within the Natchez Trace Collection, varying in size from one manuscript page to hundreds of thousands of documents. The following is a list of some of the most important of those collections that relate to areas outside of the region immediately surrounding the city of Natchez:

The Basil G. Kiger Papers (2 feet 8 inches; 1841–1885) document the workings of Kiger's plantation Buena Vista, located north of Vicksburg; Basil Kiger's wife, Carrie, was the niece of Mississippi and California politician William Gwinn, so there are some of Gwinn's letters in the collection.

The Chamberlain-Hyland-Gould Family Papers (1 foot; 1820s–1870s) pertain to the family plantation in Warren County, Mississippi, and the families' support of Oakland College.

The William L. Sharkey Papers (3 inches; 1830s–1860s) relate to the activities of the prominent Mississippi lawyer, jurist, Whig political activist, and United States senator; mainly business and legal records.

The Crutcher-Shannon Family Papers (5 inches; 1822–1905) relate to the family affairs of William and Emily Crutcher and Marmaduke Shannon of Vicksburg. The Crutcher letters include many written by William from Civil War battlefields and several written by Emily providing details about the siege of Vicksburg. Shannon, Emily's father, was publisher of the *Vicksburg Daily Whig* and an antisecessionist. The collection complements the Phillip Crutcher Collection from the same period at the Mississippi Department of Archives and History.

The Judge John Dutton Papers (6 inches; 1789–1850s) are the papers of a leading jurist in Plaquemines Parish, Louisiana; the collection includes much material pertaining to slavery in the parish.

The J. J. Cowan Papers (2 inches; 1830s–1870s) relate to the life of a leading Vicksburg cotton broker and officer in the Confederate army.

The John J. Bowie Collection (1 inch; 1810s–1830s) documents slave trade and land speculation activities in Louisiana and Mississippi of a brother of Alamo martyr Jim Bowie.

The Dr. Rowland Chambers Collection (2 inches; 1840s–1860s) concerns the work of an itinerant dentist in Vicksburg, Mississippi, and Madison Parish, Louisiana. Chambers' diary is preserved in the manuscripts collection at Louisiana State University.

The Vick Family Collection (2 inches; 1815–1840s) relates to the legal affairs of Newitt, Wesley, and Hartwell Vick, the founding family of Vicksburg, Mississippi.

The Austin Family Collection (15 pages; 1803, 1819, 1821) contains legal documents and letters relating to the activities of Texas colonizers Moses and Stephen F. Austin.

The John McKowen Papers (1 inch; 1840s–1850s) document the affairs of a merchant in East Feliciana Parish, Louisiana.

Other collections include papers related to the lives of hundreds of individuals active in the lower Mississippi River Valley including W. L. Balfour, Dr. H. G. Blackman, L. M. Boyce, James N. Brown, Arthur Carney, T. J. Chamberlain, William C. C. Claiborne, Joseph Davis, William Dearmond, F. H. Farrar, Samuel Frye, George Guier, Wade Hampton, Samuel Hart, W. B. Lintot, William Lum, W. D. McAlpin, Pierce Noland, W. C. Parish, Jacob Pettit, S. S. Prentiss, F. Skipworth, Murray Smith, John Steele, Nathaniel Williams, General James A. Wilkinson, and many others.

In addition, there are several large collections that the collector organized under general topics rather than individuals or families. These collections have yet to be analyzed properly, but they most certainly contain material pertaining to the Natchez area. They include:

The Natchez Trace Steamboat Collection (2 ft. 4 in.; 1806–1925) contains miscellaneous steamboat receipts, ledgers, documents, and other material related to commerce on the lower Mississippi River.

The Slavery Collection (3 feet; 1790s–1860s) contains legal documents, bills of sale, lists, indentures, manumission papers, runaway slave records, and other materials related to almost every aspect of the institution of slavery in Mississippi, Louisiana, and other states.

The Civil War and Reconstruction Collection (1.5 feet; 1860s) contains Confederate soldiers' letters, "guard and picket" passes, printed military orders, Confederate government printed forms, amnesty oaths, Freedman's Bureau forms, Reconstruction government documents and printed orders, and other material related to those events in Mississippi and Louisiana.

The Business Collection (12 feet; 1790s–1900s) contains ledgers, account books, legal documents, inventories, receipts, and miscellaneous material related to merchants, cotton factors, and other business activities in the lower Mississippi River Valley. Unfortunately, many of the ledgers are unidentified.

The Photograph Collection (3 feet; 1855–1920) contains tintypes, carte de visites, glass-plate negatives, and other photographic forms; predominantly portraits of planters and their extended families, some taken by antebellum portrait photographers in New Orleans. Many of these are unidentified.

The Sheet Music Collection (4,000 pieces; 1840s–1900s) contains commercially published lyrics and music richly illustrated and useful for documenting nineteenth-century popular culture. Many are scarce imprints; some are rare.

The Newspaper Collection (1806–1938) contains approximately 175 newspaper titles from more than sixty cities in nineteen states, the District of Columbia, Canada, and Great Britain; some are single issues only, but several others consist of significant runs, including papers from Natchez, Port Gibson, Jackson, Vicksburg, Canton, Fayette, Okolona, Rolling Fork, and Copiah County, Mississippi; and Baton Rouge, Lake Providence, New Orleans, Iberville, Pointe Coupee, and Richmond, Louisiana.

The Pamphlet Collection (1790s–1900s) contains several thousand items, consisting of a wide variety of pamphlet literature including government documents, college catalogs, mail order catalogs, political and religious tracts, and an assortment of almanacs, agricultural publications, scientific brochures, and other publications.

The Ephemera Collection (approximately 1,000 pieces; 1800s–1890) includes an assortment of broadsides pertaining to miscellaneous social, business, educational, political, military, and religious events.

The Natchez Trace Collection also includes a large body of manuscripts relating directly to the history of the city of Natchez and the surrounding countryside. By the spring of 1987, over thirty different collections of papers of individuals who resided in or near Natchez during the first half of the nineteenth century had been identified. Among these are small collections of papers related to the activities of the Minor family (1783–1852), Governor John A. Quitman (1820s–1860s), the wealthy planter Stephen Duncan (father and son, mostly the latter), and the Natchez merchant and alderman William J. Voss (1802–1811).

In addition, among a large collection of ledger books are a few individual ledgers of direct importance to Natchez. These include the constitution and minute book of the Natchez Relief and Hose Company (1840–1853), which has detailed reports of fires that the volunteer company had to fight. Also of interest are two log books documenting the arrival of individual boats at Natchez Landing, 1833–1840. These volumes record the hour and date of arrival, names of boat and master, point of origin and destination, and an intriguing section in which remarks could be recorded about the boat. For example, in 1839, written in the "remarks" section for different boats are such comments as "lots of women," "running like the devil," "400 U.S. troops for Florida," and "full load at big prices."

Other collections of note include the Charles Backus Dana Papers, the Jenkins Family Collection, and the Benjamin L. C. Wailes Papers. The Reverend Charles B. Dana served as the rector of Trinity Episcopal Church following the Civil War. Before coming to Natchez, Dana was rector of Christ Episcopal Church in Alexandria, Virginia, where he was a close friend of Robert E. Lee. Unfortunately, although the Reverend Dana was an influential religious leader, his chief claim to fame has been as the father of Dick Dana, the so-called wild man of Natchez who resided in what eventually became known as Goat Castle and who became nationally known because of his involvement in a bizarre murder episode in Natchez in 1932.[1] Perhaps the discovery of Reverend Dana's papers (11 inches) will shift some historical attention from the son back to the father.

The Jenkins Family Collection (5 inches) consists of papers related to the activities of the son and daughter of the famous planter and horticulturalist John C. Jenkins. The elder Jenkins and his wife died of yellow fever in the 1850s, leaving as orphans their son, John F., and their daughter, Alice. Although there is some John C. Jenkins material, such as the book listing his slaves by name in 1842, the collection largely documents the lives of Alice and John F. after the death of their parents. John F. served in the Army of Tennessee as a teen-ager and attended Washington College in Lexington, Virginia, after the war. He eventually took charge of his father's plantations and expanded his family property well beyond his inheritance. He owned two plantations in Adams County, one being the famous Elgin.[2] The collection includes many letters that this younger Jenkins wrote to his guardian while at Washington College. For example, in a letter dated December 18, 1867, he writes, "Our college is flourishing as usual, the students probably number about 400 and our faculty has had some eminent additions. Can you send me any money?" Alice, his sister, seems to have been a social sensation in Natchez in her younger years. The collection is full of the kind of ephemera (such as calling cards and invitations to soirées) that a socially active young girl would have accumulated in mid-nineteenth-century Natchez. In addition, the collection includes estate receipts documenting Alice's seemingly insatiable need for clothing, furniture, and notions from New Orleans throughout the 1860s. Alice Jenkins' receipts provide details about prices, availability of consumer goods during and after the war, and the names and locations of a variety of New Orleans and Natchez merchants.

The Benjamin L. C. Wailes Collection (2 inches) is small but substantive. Wailes, of course, is one of Natchez' best-known historical figures because of Charles S. Sydnor's biography, *A Gentleman of the Old Natchez Region*.[3] His many activities include his service as an influential trustee of Jefferson College in nearby Washington. There are, for example, several letters written to Wailes by persons wishing to join the faculty. Among these is a letter dated June 16, 1850, written by Ashbel Green from San Augustine, Texas, which presented his detailed four-page plan for Jefferson College that he would implement if the trustees would agree to appoint him president. Green proposed to Wailes that "the discipline will be military. Every pupil must wear a uniform and attend daily drills . . . one month of vacation will be spent in camp. We hope to make soldiers of our students and fit them for command if emergencies require it. We hope to build up . . . a Military Institute in no respect inferior to West Point . . . and to satisfy the South that the brains have not *all* gone North." The trustees apparently agreed because Green was subsequently hired. The Wailes papers will be a valuable supplement to collections of his now at Louisiana State and Duke universities.

The scope of the Natchez Trace Collection is wide indeed, touching on almost every aspect of historical studies. But there are nine collections that stand out as potentially the most valuable of the more than one hundred distinct groups of material. These nine include the largest collections in the Natchez Trace holdings. They relate predominantly to the Natchez area itself, and much of the material was generated before 1830: the papers of Natchez attorneys Robert H. Adams, J. B. Maxwell, George Winchester, and Josiah Winchester; the papers of planter Richard T. Archer of Anchuca Plantation in Claiborne County; the papers of Gabriel Tichenor, head cashier of the Bank of Mississippi; the papers of James C. Wilkins, a leading financier, politican, and merchant; the papers of Abram Barnes, a financier and planter; and a collection organized and labeled by the collector as the "Colonial Archives."

65

This last collection, the "Colonial Archives," consists of approximately three linear feet of French- and Spanish-language manuscripts documenting legal and administrative affairs in the period dating from the late 1770s until the late 1790s. Although considerable work remains to be done before much is known about this collection, most of these documents apparently deal predominantly with mundane bureaucratic affairs during the Spanish colonial era. Nevertheless, the most famous names of that period—including Gálvez, Gayoso, Minor, Carondelet, Grand-Pré, and Miro—are scattered throughout the Colonial Archives. Many of these colonial documents are official directives issued from New Orleans concerning legal affairs. For example, one document, dated August 4, 1796, is from Baron de Carondelet, the governor-general of Louisiana, to Manuel Gayoso de Lemos, governor of Natchez, directing Gayoso to order Don Esteban Minor, adjutant commander of Natchez, to pay a debt Minor owed to a Señora Carlota Fasende. Carondelet writes that "Minor must be required to pay the debt *immediately* or have the equivalent amount seized from his assets within 10 days and pay 25 pesos in court costs." Many other directives relate to disputes over land titles.

The Abram Barnes Collection (1.5 linear feet) consists almost entirely of documents generated in the pre-1830 period. Barnes moved to Mississippi in 1802 when he was eighteen years old. He acquired extensive landholdings and a sizable personal fortune before his death in 1830.[4] Barnes' papers include a large collection of legal records and receipts documenting his varied business activities. The collection should deepen understanding of the economic history of the Natchez area during the first third of the nineteenth century.

Of all the materials in the Natchez Trace Collection, the James C. Wilkins Papers may prove to have the greatest impact on Natchez historiography. Colonel Wilkins, a native of Pennsylvania, migrated to the Mississippi region in 1805. For most of the period from 1810 until 1849, Wilkins was one of the most important financiers in the area, chiefly through his vast operations as a cotton factor and money lender. In his history of Mississippi, J. F. H. Claiborne claims that Wilkins "controlled for a long time the commerce of Mississippi, and nearly all the cotton it produced." His mercantile activities included highly successful partnerships with John Linton and William Kenner of New Orleans. Wilkins accumulated several plantations through foreclosure and speculation. Most of his land was outside of Adams County, but in 1812 he owned 4,678 acres and 214 slaves in the county. He married well; his first wife was Adam Bingaman's daughter and his second wife was Esteban Minor's daughter. Wilkins also commanded the Natchez Rifles at the Battle of New Orleans, where his heroism and leadership attracted the attention of General Andrew Jackson. The two became lifelong friends, although Wilkins became a Whig late in life. Colonel Wilkins was deeply involved in Mississippi politics. He was a member of the territorial legislature and served as a delegate to the state constitutional convention in 1817, where he was among the leaders. Wilkins helped organize the so-called Natchez Junto, a nominally Jacksonian political club which tried to maintain Natchez' dominance in Mississippi politics. He ran for the United States Congress in 1830 but was defeated easily by Franklin Plummer. Wilkins also spearheaded the movement in 1830 to create the Planter's Bank in Natchez and he served as its first president.[5]

James Wilkins was directly involved in an impressive number of key developments in the history of the Natchez region. His papers in the Natchez Trace Collection appear to relate to many if not most of his wide-ranging affairs. Measuring over 3 feet, 9 inches, the Wilkins papers include letters from many of the most important people in the old Natchez District. The letters from Linton and Kenner in New Orleans provide extremely useful information on business activities and economic conditions in that port and elsewhere, according to Morton Rothstein, who has had an opportunity to look at the collection. Rothstein has also discovered an interesting group of letters from Nathaniel Evans, at Fort Adams, dealing with the building of the Natchez Trace in the 1801–1804 period. For example, in a letter dated December 20, 1801, Evans writes Wilkins that "the troops have not yet moved from this place [Fort Adams]. They will commence cutting the road at the Boundary line between us and Spain and will not get up as high as Natches until the beginning of February."

Many of the items in Wilkins' papers relate to political affairs. In one important letter dated May 20, 1830, Gerard Brandon, former governor of Mississippi, warns Wilkins, a candidate for Congress that year, about politicking in Jacksonian America. Brandon feared Wilkins' opponents "will represent you to the people as a man of domineering wealth, a member of the Natchez aristocracy and will not hesitate to call you a Federalist of the old school and some who call themselves of the Jackson party will take exception to your attention to Mr. Clay whilst at Natchez." Brandon, cognizant of the new political mores, advised Wilkins of "the necessity of your taking a general tour of the state. . . . It is not necessary that you should . . . visit many of the people at their houses, but those people feel themselves neglected and in fact insulted unless a candidate pays their county the compliment of a visit." Brandon also advised Wilkins "if you can possibly dispense with your servant in your route it is all important that you do so." It is not known if Wilkins heeded Brandon's wise advise, but he did lose the election.

The Natchez Trace Collection also has an extensive group of papers belonging to Gabriel Tichenor, head cashier of the Bank of Mississippi. This massive collection measures 15 linear feet and covers the period from 1808 to the 1830s. The position of head cashier was one of critical importance and, therefore, Tichenor is a key figure in the history of the Bank of Mississippi, which was the dominant financial institutional force in the state for more than twenty-five years. We know little about Tichenor himself. Apparently a native of New Jersey, he served as cashier for nearly the entire history of the bank. His daughter Elizabeth was a leader of the Female Charitable Society, the principal ladies' organization in territorial Natchez.[6] Tichenor was closely associated with the influential Dr. Stephen Duncan, who was the bank's president for several years. Tichenor's papers contain an extensive amount of material documenting the internal operations of the bank and general economic conditions throughout Mississippi during the first three decades of the nineteenth century. The Tichenor Papers include loan records, bank share certificates, powers of attorney, promissory notes, and monthly reports of funds on hand from the branch banks. In addition, there is correspondence to and from Dr. Duncan in his position as president, correspondence with bankers in New Orleans and New York, correspondence related to personnel matters within the bank, job applications, and letters from persons outside the state seeking help with collecting debts from Natchez citizens. There is much information about the buying and selling of slaves and the development of the cotton plantation economy in the 1810s and 1820s. The financial records of such prominent men as Benjamin L. C. Wailes, Dr. Duncan, Esteban Minor, Levin Covington, James C. Wilkins, Abram Barnes, H. G. Runnels, Edward Turner, James Girault, and Adam Bingaman, among others, can be found throughout the collection. Many of these documents include news unrelated to purely financial affairs. For example, in a note dated September 15, 1830, written from Woodville, Levin R. Marshall concludes a mundane message about a bank deposit with a postscript alluding to an epidemic: "Our county is becoming more healthy. I believe I am the greatest sufferer at present, however. My little son has been very ill for some days and I have two grown servants quite sick, one not expected to recover." The Tichenor Papers should provide a crucial complement to the collections of the Bank of Mississippi at the Mississippi Department of Archives and History and at Louisiana State University.

The premier collection documenting the activities of a major planter in the Natchez Trace Collection are the papers of Richard T. Archer (1790–1910). Archer, who lived near Port Gibson in Claiborne County, married Ann Barnes, the daughter of Abram Barnes. Archer was originally from Amelia County, Virginia, and his collection includes letters full of information about conditions in the Old Dominion during the antebellum years. Richard Archer was also related to Branch T. Archer, a leader in the Texas Revolution and a diplomat for the Republic of Texas.[7] There are several letters from Branch to Richard conveying news about events in Texas. The Archer Papers are an important source for social history, rich with information about slavery, child-raising, diet, architecture, women's roles and activities, education, crime, popular culture, health, and religion. Archer was close to the elite Natchez families in Adams County and corresponded extensively with them. He was a tireless writer of letters to editors of major southern journals, and drafts of his writings on national politics in the collection reveal his ardent support of secession. He wrote many anonymous letters to the editors of Mississippi newspapers, especially during the controversy swirling around the Compromise of 1850. He frequently signed these letters "plain farmer" or "rustic" although, as Shearer Davis Bowman has pointed out, Archer owned nearly four hundred slaves in Claiborne and Holmes counties just before the Civil War. In a letter drafted in September, 1850, meant for circulation in Adams County, Archer argued that the South could legally withdraw from the Union because "the Constitution was an experiment" and was never intended to be "perpetual." Archer was a friend of Felix Huston, a Natchez attorney who briefly participated in the Texas Revolution and in the military affairs of the Republic of Texas.[8] There are several Huston letters in the collection.

Because of the litigation over confused land titles stemming from conflicting colonial grants as well as chaotic land speculation activities, Natchez attracted an inordinate number of attorneys. Appropriately, the Natchez Trace Collection includes the papers of several lawyers. The most significant of these are the papers of Robert H. Adams, John B. Maxwell, and George and Josiah Winchester.

Robert Adams was among the leading attorneys in the city throughout the 1820s. He was active politically and was elected United States senator in 1830 but died soon after arriving in Washington.[9] His collection consists of approximately one hundred letters relating to his law practice, with a special emphasis on his legal work with the slave trade. John B. Maxwell was not as prominent as Adams, but he had an active legal business in Natchez from the late 1830s through the 1840s. His collection consists of approximately one hundred letters plus some probate records. Maxwell and Adams were both heavily involved in probate matters, as were the Winchesters and other attorneys whose papers are in the Natchez Trace Collection.

The Winchester Papers measure over 15 linear feet. They document the careers of Judge George Winchester and his nephew Josiah; the papers relate to political, economic, legal, and cultural affairs in the Natchez area from 1817 until the late 1880s. Both uncle and nephew were among the most influential citizens in Natchez throughout this period, and their papers promise to be extraordinarily important. The erudite George Winchester was born in 1793 in Salem, Massachusetts; he graduated from Harvard and read law with the distinguished Supreme Court justice Joseph Story. He moved to Natchez in 1817 and began what soon became a prosperous law practice, representing many of the Natchez area's leading planters in the courts. In the 1820s George Winchester became a judge of the Supreme Court of Mississippi. Characterized by one contemporary as an ultra states-rights man, Winchester was an ardent admirer of John C. Calhoun. Politically a Whig, he ran unsuccessfully for governor in 1829.

Winchester presided over the Southern Rights Convention held at Jackson in 1849 to oppose the antislavery movement. He was the author of the main address and all of the resolutions adopted at the convention. A year before that event, Winchester was the head of Adams County's Rough and Ready Club, which served as the local campaign organization for Zachary Taylor's presidential race.[10] He was close to many of the leading citizens of the Natchez area, but perhaps his closest friend was the prominent planter and resident of Briars, William Burr Howell. Winchester served for several years as the personal tutor of Howell's daughter, Varina, who would later marry Jefferson Davis. In fact, Judge Winchester played a role in the courtship of Jefferson and Varina. Varina says in her famous biography of her husband, "The Judge was one of the great influences in my life." He was, she says, "my childish ideal of the Great—heart, eminent, and incorruptible; his charity as wide as the horizon."[11]

The Judge died in 1851, but his nephew Josiah continued to practice law until his death in 1888. Although Josiah never equaled his uncle in political power, he was, nevertheless, an important figure in Natchez history. Josiah was also a native of Salem, Massachusetts, and studied law in Boston with Rufus Choate. He joined his uncle in Natchez sometime in the 1830s, bringing with him views about the nature of the Union that differed radically from his uncle. Josiah was a staunch Union man and, after his uncle's death, wrote a pamphlet, *To the Thinking Men of the South,* which argued against secession. The voters of Adams County sent him to the Mississippi secession convention as a pro-Union delegate. During the war, Josiah steadfastly refused to help the Confederacy, and after Union troops occupied Natchez, he was known as one of the town's leading cooperationists.

Josiah's wife was Margaret Sprague, the daughter of Howell Sprague, cashier of the Agricultural Bank. As one example of the linkage among Natchez families, their daughter Louisa married John F. Jenkins. Josiah, who was probate judge of Adams County for several years, had served as young Jenkins' guardian. For a novice at Natchez history, these family interrelationships can get confusing. For example, Margaret Sprague Winchester was Varina Howell Davis' cousin.[12]

Obviously, the papers of the two Winchesters hold much promise for casting new light on a multitude of historical issues. The collection is full of correspondence with other leading citizens of Natchez. For example, a letter dated January 29, 1846, written to George by William Burr Howell from the Briars, complains that "I have not been favored thus far with a line from Jefferson [Davis, his new son-in-law], though I certainly did count upon at least a partial correspondence during his stay at the seat of government—if only to say he recollected we were related." Another letter to George, written by Senator George Poindexter from Washington, D.C., dated September 2, 1842, deals with larger political matters. Poindexter informs Judge Winchester, who was the senator's attorney in Natchez, that "Congress has just closed a long and boisterous session. They have fixed on the highest tariff ever known in this country which I fear will utterly annihilate the Whigs in the Southern states where these high taxes will chiefly fall." Poindexter goes on to say that "overgrown capitalists in the north . . . engaged in the manufacture of domestic goods" were to blame for this situation. In addition, the collection includes draft manuscripts of George's judicial decisions and an extensive group of records related to his and Josiah's legal practice. They also received many letters from relatives in Massachusetts that have much information about conditions in New England spanning more than fifty years.

Another important component of the Winchester Papers are the letters Josiah's wife Margaret wrote to her husband during his frequent trips to Jackson. The letters are well written and filled with details about her daily life as a wife, mother, and socially prominent woman in antebellum Natchez. During one of her husband's absences in 1854, she writes to him from their home The Elms:

> My dear husband,
>
> I fear I shall be quite a nervous lady by the time you get back. One night while awake with Mary I heard a terrible rumbling, something like the 'silent thunder' so vividly described in the eruption of Vesuvius. Then came a crash that shook the house. I made our son get up and take a light in the parlor where the noise came from. There was a large piece of plaster that had fallen from the ceiling just over the card table. It is real mercy it had not fallen while the chilren were dancing. Mr. Carket is to come out tomorrow and if he says it must come off I'll just let it alone till you come home."

She went on to tell Josiah in a letter two days later "that old Railey cow took a run at me . . . and made me take to Calhoun's fence in fine style, she gave me a dreadful backache, but after a good *crying fit* it felt much better. Write whenever you have time, but don't deprive yourself of your sleep to do it, I'll try to be satisfied to hear from you once a week. . . . Your loving wife, Missy."

Margaret's letter is but one of the variety of sources in the Natchez Trace Collection that will have value for social historians. Although the collection has much to contribute to traditional historical research in politics, military affairs, and the administration of government, it should make its greatest impact in the now firmly rooted field of the "new" social history—the historical concern for studying the lives, institutions, activities, beliefs, and superstitions of ordinary people, those people previously invisible and considered inarticulate: workers, housewives, children, the aged, black and ethnic groups, and people from all levels of the lower and middle classes. The new social history depends on nontraditional sources and the use of conventional sources in new ways. For example, courthouse documents of every type—police records, wills, estate inventories, diaries, photographs and other visual records, ephemera, and lists of all sorts are absolutely essential to the work of scholars in the field of social history. The collection is especially rich in such sources.

The documents in the Natchez Trace Collection convey a vivid impression of the vanished world in which the people of the Old Natchez District worked and played, lived and died. Ledgers record the goods yeoman farmers needed, the prices they had to pay, and the indebtedness they created. An obstetrician's book reveals details about birthing and infant mortality. A diary preserves the events of a young girl's adolescence. Estate inventories list the household furnishings, clothing, and other property of planters and small farmers alike. A manumission paper proves the freedom of a female slave named Lizzie whereas the judicial record of another indicates a sentence of ten lashes "well laid on" for thirty consecutive days for resisting his master. Bills of sale document the size of slave families, the prices individuals commanded, and other details such as the loss of fingers and toes and the presence of scars on faces and backs. One bill of sale states: "May 15, 1848, a slave named Anthony was sold for $600.00. Anthony is 27 years old, mulatto, a little bald. He is strong and athletic. He is 5 ft. 10 inches."

Because of its size and comprehensiveness—almost every aspect of life and culture is covered—the Natchez Trace Collection will help scholars make significant contributions to the understanding of the development of one of the most important regions in the United States in the first half of the nineteenth century.

Notes

1. Sim C. Callon and Carolyn Vance Smith, *The Goat Castle Murder* (Natchez: Plantation, 1985), 18–19.

2. *Goodspeed's Biographical and Historical Memoirs of Mississippi* (2 vols.; Chicago: Goodspeed, 1891), I, 1020–21.

3. Charles S. Sydnor, *A Gentleman of the Old Natchez Region: Benjamin L. C. Wailes* (Durham: Duke University Press, 1938).

4. *Goodspeed*, I, 309.

5. J. F. H. Claiborne, *Mississippi as a Province, Territory and State, with Biographical Notices of Eminent Citizens* (1884; repr. Baton Rouge: Louisiana State University Press, 1964), 345–46, 353. See also Edwin Arthur Miles, *Jacksonian Democracy in Mississippi*

(Chapel Hill: University of North Carolina Press, 1960), 13, 30–32; Clayton D. James, "Antebellum Natchez" (Ph.D. dissertation, University of Texas, 1964), 110–11.

6. James, "Antebellum Natchez," 159.

7. *Goodspeed*, I, 310.

8. Shearer Davis Bowman, "Slaveholders and the Constitution: Attitudes in Mississippi and Virginia During the Secession Crisis of 1860–61" (MSS., Department of History, University of Texas at Austin, 1987), 14–15; Walter P. Webb (ed.), *The Handbook of Texas* (2 vols.; Austin: Texas State Historical Association, 1952), I, 63, 869.

9. James D. Lynch, *The Bench and Bar of Mississippi* (New York: E. J. Hale and Sons, 1881), 24, 25.

10. Robert E. May, *John A. Quitman: Old South Crusader* (Baton Rouge: Louisiana State University Press, 1985), 24. See also Lynch, *Bench and Bar of Mississippi*, 100–101; Claiborne, *Mississippi as a Province*, 471; James, "Antebellum Natchez," 304.

11. Harnett T. Kane, *Natchez on the Mississippi* (New York: Morrow, 1947), 238, 240.

12. *Goodspeed*, I, 1021.

Mapping the Foundations
of the Old Natchez District:
The Wilton Map of 1774

M ILTON B. N EWTON , J R.

Introduction

In 1763, Great Britain gained possession of the formerly French territory lying along the left bank of the Mississippi as far downstream as Bayou Manchac. This expanse includes as its southern extremity what some have called the Old Natchez District. By 1770, British settlers had well begun to receive grants in the District, and, under the rules governing the taking of such grants, surveys were to be made of each tract. The engineer, or surveyor, William Wilton conducted some of the requisite surveys, recording the claims on his map entitled "Part of the River Mississippi From Manchac up to the River Yazous." With Wilton's map, we have the documentation of the arrival of tangible British order upon the land of the Old Natchez District.

Land Law and Public Order

From a geographical perspective, royal colonial claims to vast tracts of North America lack something of the earthy quality that geographers seek and enjoy. The claims may or may not ultimately gain credibility and force in the landscape. We need only recall the many cessions of territory that have left little more than a few names on the land. With the establishment of the cadaster, however, geographers recognize nearly indelible marks upon the land. Once established, the lines delineating the original grants of property generally endure, and only an event comparable to the one that made them possible can eradicate these

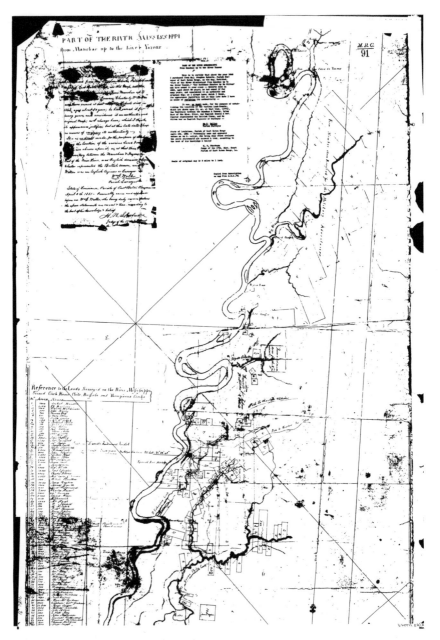

Wilton's map, Part of the River Mississippi from Manchac up to the River Yazous. Courtesy of Mississippi Department of Archives and History.

landscape marks. All subsequent land transactions, whether division or agglomeration, take place in terms of the original surveys. How could it be otherwise? How could the historic development of the landscape have gone forward, except in terms of known and established reference points and lines? As it turns out, it could have been different.

From the perspective of incoming Europeans and, indeed, largely from that of the indigenous Indians, the land of North America in general and the Old Natchez District in particular was an undifferentiated mass. There simply were no or very few known and established points and lines in the Old Natchez District before the arrival of Europeans. There were generalized, vague areas that were more or less dominated and controlled by one village or confederation or another, but boundaries, in any strict sense, were practically nonexistent.

Indeed, had Europeans of several centuries earlier conquered the Old Natchez District, they too would have lacked any clear concepts of landed property, strictly defined. Newly acquired lands would have been given by the Crown as fiefs subject to faithful and successful captains of the conquest, as, for example, had been the case in the Spanish conquest of what is now Latin America. In the Britain of the preceding feudal period, "The folkland became the king's land; the soldier was a landowner instead of the landowner being a soldier."

In fact, some of the land was indeed granted in a manner similar to the old system. "Mandamus" grants, given to distinguished personages, ranged in excess of 2,000 acres. Only 14 (plus, perhaps, 4 more) such large grants, however, were listed in Wilton's register and other sources.[1] Much like the empresario grants of the Spaniards, these entailed the placement on the land of one free, white, Protestant settler for every hundred acres; few of the mandamus grants actually endured because the grantees failed to meet the terms of the grants. Holders of mandamus grants in the Old Natchez District simply did not earn the right to continue in title. As a consequence, the lands covered by the larger of these mandamus grants reverted to the Crown. The "crown," as it turned out, would be Spain.

Under a second program of dispersing land and promoting settlement, "royal order" grants were given to "reduced officers" mustered out of royal services after the Seven Years War. In the region covered by Wilton's map, 39 such grants were made.[2] They generally included 2,000 or 3,000 acres, although some of 50, 150, 300, and 500 acres were made. Several men held title to land under both mandamus and royal order grants.

77

Beginning in 1709 and reaching its peak between 1765 and 1785, the inclosure movement in Britain converted large amounts of common land into freehold land or its near approximation. Thus began to culminate a long fought effort to gain rights that came close to what we would see as a right to real property held in fee simple. Moreover, the peak of the fever of acts of inclosure occurred just at the time that the Old Natchez District was being colonized.

It is one of the aspects of the New World experience that the Europeans arriving in the District, among other places, came with the then currently popular British ideas about private property. In particular in the case of the Old Natchez District, those of the philosophers in the Scottish school of rationalism held the day and gained expression through the ministers of the Georges. In the *tabula rasa* of North America, the new ideas could gain unfettered dominance; no recognized, entrenched, competing system stood in the way.

As a result, in the third program of land disbursement, the very invitation to settle the new conquests took the form of offers of "head-rights," or "family rights," which granted to each head of a household the right to claim a tract of land, proportioned according to number of dependents; heads of families could be male or female, and members of the head's household could be free or slave. The head could also purchase ("purchase right") additional land up to a maximum of 1,000 acres. The head had, however, actually to settle the land and give evidence of such actual occupancy and use, primarily by building a dwelling house of 20 by 16 feet.

While many may hold an image of the grants of the British period as being princely in size, the record of the Wilton map and associated documents denies such a conception. Three-quarters of all grants amounted to less than 2,000 acres (less than three square miles), while only an eighth embraced more than 1,000 acres. Indeed, three-tenths held between 500 and 999 acres, most in that group being 500 or 600 acres. Only seven of 335 grants held 10,000 or more acres. Less than a tenth comprised 200 acres or less. From these figures, it is clear that the New World experience in the Old Natchez District included, also, a reasonably general distribution of land to actual producers. Eventually, the land had to be surveyed, for nothing can actually exist unless it "takes place." The act of severance of the actual soil from the generalized and undivided possession of the sovereign required in principle and eventually in fact the specific delineation of some definite parcel of land. The historic and geographic singularity of *taking place* was mir-

Table 1. Distribution of British land grants by size, type, and area. Source: Wells 1966 and Wilton 1774.

Size, acres		North of Lat. 31 M	RO	Other	South of Lat. 31 M	RO	Other	Supplementary M	RO	Other	Total
50	– 99			4						3	7
100	– 199			5			5	2	10		22
200	– 499			8			12		15		35
500	– 999			31	2		29	3	36		101
1000	– 1499		12	29	1		32	8	33		115
1500	– 1999		1	3			1		3		8
2000	– 4999		4	5	2	2	3		6		22
5000	– 9999	1	2		5			1			4
10,000	– 19,999										5
20,000	and larger	2									2
Not classed							1			3	4
Total		3	19	85	7	5	83	1	13	109	325

rored in similar singularities in law and surveying. The parcel did not exist until it had been allocated, delimited, and demarcated (to use political geographers' terms); that once done, the parcel endured, generally to our time.

In this way, civil order gained actual standing on the land; it was much more than merely the beginnings of British engravings on the surface of the Natchez District earth: just as the Indian and feudal land systems gave tangible expression to the values of their founders, the new land grants became the landscape of belief of the new order. So too would the Spanish and American systems.

Wilton's Map

William Wilton was himself a colonist and land claimant; his grant of 200 acres lay on the bank of the Mississippi, opposite Pointe Coupee, near the juncture of the borders of present East Baton Rouge, East Feliciana, and West Feliciana parishes. Wilton would eventually claim additional lands before the U.S. Commissioners charged with evaluating such claims. His own grant lay a scant five miles from one of Elias Durnford and ten miles from that of George Gauld (1778) on Thompsons Creek, both historic cartographers of the region. Wilton, in addition to being a government surveyor, was a royal official and a merchant with operations in Pensacola, as well as in the District.[3]

As an engineer, or surveyor, Wilton prepared at least two general maps of the new head rights. One, dated 1770, bearing the title "Plan of the

River Mississippi from the River Yazous to the River Iberville," denotes fewer grants along the Mississippi and none along the Amite. The second, dated 1774, Wilton titled "Part of the River Mississippi from Manchac up to the River Yazous for Governor Chester."(In the title block, "for Governor Chester" was added later.) This map presents what purports to be a much fuller picture of the British head rights in the District. It is the map that concerns us here.

Historic Background. At the present time, it seems that only copies of the Wilton map exist. According to marginal notes, the original was taken into the collections of the Mississippi River Commission, although recent efforts at the Commission library yielded the report that the original map cannot be found. Copies are known to repose in the Mississippi Department of Archives and History and in the Hill Memorial Library and the Cartographic Information Center (CIC) at Louisiana State University. The latter two copies differ from each other in that each lacks certain repairs and restorations that appear in the other.

The copies bear on their upper left corners two annexed documents, the second a typescript rendition of the first. In full, the typescript reads:

PART OF THE RIVER MISSISSIPPI
From Manchac up to the River Yazous

This is to certify that about the year 1848 I purchased from Maj. Stephen Roberts, Parish Surveyor of East Baton Rouge, an Old Map, Entitled, "Part of the River Mississippi from Manchac up to the River Yazous," "for Governor Chester by Wm Wilton" and have owned it ever since—Roberts died in 1863, aged about 80 years; he had owned it for many years, and considered it an authentic and original map; as I always have; which I think, its appearance justifies; but at this late date I have no means of *veryfying* its authenticity—

It was, *no doubt* made, for the purpose of establishing the location of the various Land Grants, which are shown upon it; as, at that time, (1774), the Territory between the Manchac & Yazous, lying East of the Miss. River, was English domain & Gov. Chester represented the British Crown, and Wm Wilton was an English Engineer or Surveyor—

Wm   G.   Waller
Parish Surveyor

State of Louisiana, Parish of East Baton Rouge April 4th, 1881—Personally came and appeared before me Wm G. Waller, who being duly sworn declares the above statements are correct & true, according to the best of his knowledge and belief

H, N, Sherburn
Judge of the 17th. Dist. Court
Parish of East Baton Rouge, La.

Scale of original map is 2 miles to 1 inch.

Copied from description
on map File M.R.C./91

Upon William Waller's affidavit depends nearly all that is known of the map's credentials, other than the map's inherent contents.

Description of the Map.   The copy of Wilton's map on file in the CIC measures about 70 by 27.5 inches. It is apparently a print from a negative made of the original, both presumably in the MRC library. The original was drawn on several sheets of paper that were later joined and mounted on cloth. The edges of the original, particularly the bottom, sustained damaged which shows clearly in the print. Even so, traces of a border and neatline appear on all four sides, showing that the print is that of a complete map. The two southern corners of the map have been obliterated by a stain, apparently spilled ink.

In addition to the two copies of the historic validation document in the northwest corner and the label "M.R.C./91" in the northeast corner, the map contains a bar scale, a compass rose, and a register of grant holders. The bar scale in the middle of the southern edge, although badly damaged, permits the determination of three miles of scaled measurement. The correctness of the assumption that the dark and light segments of the bar scale represent miles can be confirmed by comparative measurements. Such determinations show that the copy in CIC has a scale of approximately 2 miles to the inch, or 1:126,720. The 32-point compass rose occupies a prominent location in the middle of the eastern part of the map, approximately over the boundary of present Wilkinson and Amite counties.

Occupying much of the west margin of the map is a register of grant holders bearing the title "Reference to the Lands Surveyed on the River Mississippi, Second Creek, Huma Chita, Buffalo, and Thompsons Creeks." Under the title, the original column headings report "No," "Acres," and "Names:" The register (lots 1 through 202) continues southward until, at lot number 180, it disappears in the obliterations of the southwest corner. A second column of the register, in a different hand, lies east of the lower part of the first; it lists lots 222, 225, 229 through 233, 234, and 235. This second register has column heads for

Table 2. Areas and sides of square and long lots of grants of selected sizes. (The length of a "long lot" is three times its width.)

		Square Lots		Long Lots	
Acres	Sq Ft	Wide, ft	Wide, mi	Wide, ft	Wide, mi
50	2,178,000	1,475.80	0.28	852.06	0.16
100	4,356,000	2,087.10	0.40	1,204.99	0.23
200	8,712,000	2,951.61	0.56	1,704.11	0.32
500	21,780,000	4,666.90	0.88	2,694.44	0.51
600	26,136,000	5,112.34	0.97	2,951.61	0.56
640	27,878,400	5,280.00	1.00	3,048.41	0.58
1,000	43,560,000	6,600.00	1.25	3,810.51	0.72
1,525	66,429,000	8,150.40	1.54	4,705.63	0.89
2,000	87,120,000	9,333.81	1.77	5,388.88	1.02
3,000	130,680,000	11,431.54	2.17	6,600.00	1.25
10,000	435,600,000	20,871.03	3.95	12,049.90	2.28
17,400	757,944,000	27,530.78	5.21	15,894.90	3.01
20,000	871,200,000	29,516.10	5.59	17,041.13	3.23
25,600	1,115,136,000	33,393.65	6.32	19,279.83	3.65

"Lot," "Acres," and "Original Patentee." The obliterated names were reconstructed by Wells from other records of the British Public Record Office. Wells mistakenly states that a descriptive phrase, "French Plantations," which merely *describes* the right bank, is the title of the second, supplementary, and subsequent register. Similarly rendered descriptive terms also appear: e.g., "Indian Village," and "Pointe Coupee."

Beyond these registered lots, additional tracts are delineated and numbered (including those in the second register) from 203 to 250. Of these, 203 through 213 and 220 through 227 form the "New Settlement" (today, Baton Rouge). Lots 214 through 219 and 228 through 232 lie north of the land reserved for Fort Bute and the proposed town of Harwich. Lots 234 through 236 lie on St. Catherines Creek, 241 and 242 on Second Creek, 243 through 248 near the mouths of the Homochitto and Buffalo, and 250 on Boyds (Coles) Creek. Numbers 233, 237 through 240, and 249 seem to be unassigned, although they may pertain to the seven unnumbered tracts (four along Second Creek in Mississippi) that also appear on Wilton's map.

No register appears for lots numbered from 1 through 102 (Wells says, "No. 1 through No. 100"), which the map shows to lie along Bayou Manchac ("River Iberville") and the Comite and Amite rivers. While the segment of the map that contains the Amite-Manchac grants bears the same border and neatline, they do occupy one of the several patches of paper that were mounted on cloth backing to form the whole map. Lines that cross the seams between separate patches do not align, a fact showing that they were joined after having been separately drawn.

Nine of these Amite-Manchac tracts bear names of claimants, added subsequently and in different hands. Wells does not identify them as emendations. Nonetheless, he does provide 130 names of grantees whose tracts remain to be identified. Wells discovered evidence of these grants in the British records. At the northeast corner, occupying its own patch of paper, appears another numbered series of tracts "Reserved for the Military Adventurers." No register appears for this series of tracts.

Of natural features Wilton included, of course, the Mississippi from just above Les Cotes de Yazous (Vicksburg) to just below the efflux of the Mississippi into Bayou Manchac; main tributaries of the left bank include the Yazoo, the Big Black, Coles, St. Catherines, Second, Homochitto, Buffalo, Tunica, Sara, and Thompsons. On the right bank, Wilton indicates the Mississippi's junctures with the Red and the Atchafalaya, and the courses of the Comite and Amite. Along the channel of the Mississippi, he included notable islands and the names of bends and bluffs, and he attempts to indicate by hachuring the locations of bluffs along the Mississippi and its left bank tributaries. He locates other cultural features of interest, including forts at and opposite Natchez, Fort Bute, and the fort at Pointe Coupee. Additional tracts of "Reserved Land" (reserved, apparently, for public purposes) appear (by implication) at Natchez surrounding the fort, at the juncture of the Mississippi and Manchac, and at the juncture of the Amite and Manchac. A subsequent hand marked two other tracts north and east of Natchez as reserved for particular persons.

Places identified as "Indian Village" appear on the right bank above Raccourci Bend and below Manchac. On the left bank, another "Indian Village" appears just north of Fort Bute, while "Tonicas village" (mistakenly rendered by Wells and others as "Lonicoos") is shown to lie on the left bank, above Pointe Coupee.

Of no less interest are trails shown in various parts, often bearing the designation "Path." The largest number of these radiate north, east, and south from Natchez: two bear the names "Path to the Chactaw Nation" and "Path to Choctaw Six Towns." Several paths also concentrate along Second Creek. A long path extends generally southward along the Homochitto and the lower Buffalo, then following the bluffs above the Buffalo to the Rocks of Davion; from there, its course is not clear, but it probably extends to Tunica Bayou, where an overland trail descends from the northeast. Another path appears along the northern bank of the Manchac with a branch leading southward in Spanish territory. Other worn traces suggest a few other paths. These paths formed part of an extensive network of Indian trails across the South, only part of which was recorded for the District by Wilton.

Evaluation of the Map.   The CIC copy of Wilton's map is one of an altered document. Dates included in additions range from 1817 to 1831. Most of these additions occur in hands different enough from Wilton's to make recognition relatively easy.

Some of the additions, however, seem to be in the hand of Wilton. These include a note on the cutting off of Lake St. Mary in 1776: "Cut Off 1776." The probable balance of Wilton's additions consist of the tracts drawn and numbered from 203 to 250. When he prepared the plat of the Amite-Manchac claims cannot be determined, but it was probably after the main set listed in the register.

Wilton's delineation of the streams of the area covered by his map falls short of the standards that were emerging at the time. Comparison of Wilton (1774) with Durnford (1771);[4] Gauld (1778),[5] and Pittman ([1765])[6] shows that Wilton used out-of-date sources; the incidence of French phrases and terms suggests that his sources, at least in part, pre-dated the then-current field research in the region.

Wilton's map consists of at least three pieces of paper, each covering an area with its own series of numbered tracts. The patch that covers the Amite-Manchac group is drawn at a larger scale than that covering the tracts listed in the register. Moreover, its orientation is incorrect, partly because the course of Bayou Manchac, which connects the two, is incorrect: Wilton shows Manchac to run southwest to northeast when, in fact, it runs due east from the Mississippi.

Pattern of British Claims

Regardless of the shapes of the grants shown by Wilton that actually survived into the American period, the pattern of the claims provides a view of what the British settlers believed to be intrinsically worthwhile or likely to appreciate in worth. By their selection of sites, the claimants, whether speculator or settler or both, made a practical assessment of the land's probability to provide them gain, security, or both.

Relation to Natural Features.   Standing back and viewing Wilton's map from a distance gives the clear idea that the British settlers and claimants took cognizance of four main land qualities.

By far, the most important natural aspect of the District for most colonists was riparian location. Most tracts occupy sites either fronting on streams, or straddling them. Of course, the streams provided nearly the sole means of entering the area and, so, may strongly have suggested riparian sites. Of the 202 grants listed in Wilton's original register, 135 (two-thirds) fronted on the Mississippi or stood directly back of one that did. Similarly, nearly all of the 102 grants in the Amite-Manchac group occupied the stream front or the immediately-adjacent land to the back. Another 22 occupied the same kinds of sites along the lower reaches of Thompsons Creek, while 20 did so along the Homochitto-Buffalo system.

A rule governing the shapes of grants under the British regime provides one key to the claimants' evaluation of the lands that they chose. The instructions to surveyors required that, along *navigable* streams, no grant could straddle the streams and, further, that the width of such a grant could not be greater than one-third of its length. These regulations helped insure that the benefit of access to navigable water would be widely enjoyed.

Thus, while their evaluations of the smaller streams' potential for navigation may have been excessive, the shape and arrangement of the grants, nonetheless, documents their opinions and aspirations. Taking the traditional definition of *navigable* as the ability to support commerce in schooners, perhaps five claims on the Amite lay beyond the head of navigation; another dozen on the Comite probably reflected mistaken notions of the reach of schooners. These riparian grants extended westward along Bayou Manchac approximately to the mouth of Bayou Fountain, which lies a little west of the traditional head of navigation, but not implausibly so. On Thompsons Creek, if we make the historic allowance for seasonally high water, the grants reflect a correct estimation of navigability up to the present site of Jackson.

The analysis of grants of the confluence of the Homochitto and Buffalo is both more complex and more ambiguous. The Mississippi floodplain here strongly influences these two streams, and the Homochitto and Buffalo interacted in their lower courses with each other and with the waters of the Mississippi. As a consequence, our evaluation of the navigability of the Homochitto and the Buffalo would probably differ from that of eighteenth-century settlers. Nonetheless, 20 grants were sited along these streams; those fronting on the Homochitto reached as far east as the boundary between Adams and Franklin counties. Despite any reservation that we might have as to the viability of these streams as avenues of commerce, the rules governing grants on such streams were applied, leaving the burden of proof on us.

That a reasonable distinction between navigable and non-navigable streams was generally maintained can be seen in the grants along other small streams. Southeast of Natchez, claims along St. Catherines and Second creeks generally span the streams. The boundaries of those along Second Creek mostly lie perpendicular to the creek. The grants lying along St. Catherines evince a townly order, carrying on the cardinal boundary orientation of the reserve surrounding Fort Rosalie. Along both streams, we must presume, the surveyor did not judge the waters to be navigable; hence, he did not enforce the applicable rules.

These grants near Natchez, especially along Second Creek, were smaller than normal. Most of them had between 100 and 500 acres. According to a note in Wilton's hand and one in another, they also overlapped lands reserved for members of the Hutchins family. (Thomas Hutchins, a distinguished frontier officer, was the fourth cartographer holding land in the area mapped by Wilton. Hutchins later became Geographer of the United States.)

The third natural orientation feature that seems to have attracted these claimants was broken terrain. Particularly north of Baton Rouge, most grants had a hundred feet of local relief within their bounds. More especially, they generally had a bluff that overlooked a floodplain. The significance of such a site choice may have lain in the eighteenth-century tendency to place roads and trails along bluffs. Inherited perhaps from the antecedent Indian paths, such sites nonetheless provided a conveniently drained locale for both roads and homesites.

Quite at variance with others, some claimants, seemingly oblivious to the threat posed by the great river, chose to take up lands on the natural levees and even in the backswamps of the Mississippi; some of these claimants saw their lands taken away by the meandering Mississippi. Even so, all four Indian villages noted by Wilton also occupied such sites, including that of his neighbors, the Tunicas.

Relation to Indian Settlement. To review Wilton's map in the light of the known business of many of the settlers leads to yet another pattern in the British settlers' choice of sites for their claims. Trade with Indians so dominated the first years of the colony that it is not surprising to see that then present and former Indian village sites and Indian paths indexed the landscape for the colonists.

Most of the clusters of small grants lay at or near the places where

Indian paths converged or where they met the Mississippi. Naturally, such places had been or would be suitable points for locating trading operations. Thus, southeast of Natchez, south of Fort Adams, the mouth of Tunica Bayou, the mouth of Bayou Sara, the present site of Baton Rouge, and the juncture of the Mississippi and Bayou Manchac were sites that could have been expected to bring commercial contact with the Indians. At all of these points, small grants cluster, crowding in for a share of the action.

Also along Second Creek, however, the presence of a path seems to have made the sites more attractive to the British. Northeast of Natchez as well, the paths leading to the Choctaw Nation suggested locales promising to at least eight claimants. In that sector, moreover, lay a reserve of 25,000 acres once claimed by Thomas Hutchins, whose frontier experience and geographical orientation may have informed his choice.

In any event, the settling of a new land provided vast and somewhat indeterminable challenges. To find places already at least partly domesticated by humans was to discover hopeful signs. The existence of clearings, evidence of cultivation, housesites, known paths, and perhaps at least a few indigenous settlers not only eased the colonists' chore, but also assured them that, indeed, people had lived and could live in the place. Explorers in this period routinely made note of abandoned Indian villages and oldfields as evidence of the habitability of places.

Relation to French Settlement. One additional factor surely influenced some colonists' choice of sites for their claims. Opposite Bayou Sara and Thompsons Creek, Wilton shows the right bank settlements of the French at Pointe Coupee. With the terms "French Plantations" and "Pointe Coupee," as well as "Fort" and "Church," Wilton identified the main area that was then developed by the French.

As the Indian villages suggested the commercial opportunity, so did the French settlements provide such opportunities. Although such trade with Spanish territory would have been illegal, it did occur. In any case, the hope of trade with the established French planters would have increased the attractiveness of the left bank opposite Pointe Coupee.

Pattern of Surviving Claims

For any historic land claim to endure to the present, it must have negotiated the legal framework of each succeeding regime. By traditional rights, each regime required verification of rights to lands that, therefore, would not be part of crown or public domain. To be blunt, officials of the time would have wanted to know what lands remained available for distribution under their control. The matter became even more demanding during the turn of the century, when a vast number of settlers entered the District, nearly all of them seeking land.

Perfection of Claims. To carry out the procedures required by law to obtain title to land was the act, or process, of "perfecting" title. As a fairly general rule, perfected claims were honored by subsequent regimes.

British colonial law required, among other procedures, that the claimant occupy and improve the land received under the several programs. In some cases, the grantee's interest in the land could not be sold or otherwise transferred until after title had been given. Upon showing that the grant had been occupied and improved at the prescribed rate and upon completion of survey and filings, the grantee received a title. In the case of the empresario-like mandamus grants, the separate settlers brought by the grantee seem to have had to go through the perfection process.

Spanish Invasion. The British colonial administration of West Florida lasted only from 1763 to 1779; for land granting, it effectively endured only from 1770 to 1779, a mere nine years. During that period, invited settlers appeared and disappeared; some never arrived to occupy their claims; others arrived without invitation; some claimed more than they were due; finally, some legally and illegally trafficked in lands of the District.

The Spanish conquest of West Florida in 1779, in effect, caught the British settlers in the midst of a very fluid development. Spanish policy, however, recognized legitimate, perfected claims, while rejecting those that lacked clear evidence of having at least most of the requirements of perfection. Lands not included within perfected grants reverted to the Spanish Crown. Persons who had lost their lands from want of perfection, could and often did successfully file new claims under Spanish authority. At Tunica Bayou in West Feliciana Parish, for example, Oliver Pollock had bought from James Willing, who had obtained the tract from Henry Fairchild, who also held lands near Natchez; with the Spanish invasion, the title was found wanting, and the land reverted to the Crown. Carlos Trudeau acquired the land and, by apparent prearrangement, conveyed it back to Oliver Pollock.[7] The size, shape, and location of the new tract, however, differed from those of the old one.

Spanish policy also promoted the entry of new settlers, almost from any source. The Spanish apparently hoped to use land to buy settlers' loyalty, a practice also later followed in the same region by the Congress of the United States. Lands not clearly perfected were subject to redistribution, commonly with the view of entering a large number of loyal Spanish subjects. For example, in the area of Lord Eglinton's claim (29 on Wilton's map) to 2,000 acres situated immediately north of Natchez, the U.S. Commissioners reported, "The land is entirely covered by Spanish patents, being one of the most flourishing settlements in this district."[8]

American State Papers.   Upon the United States' clear acquisition of the District by the Treaty of London in 1783 and the Treaty of Madrid in 1795, the complexity of land tenure had become compounded. Added to the three types of British grant and many Spanish grants (often to persons who also held, or had lost, British grants) were several types of claim that could be filed under U.S. law. What had been crown domain became public domain; Congress had the power to dispose of lands owned by the United States, but not that owned by a private person. Technically, *public domain* does not become *public land* until it has been surveyed and identified as a specific tract in a definite place. At such time, the land, now public land, could be opened for sale to qualified settlers.

Like her colonial predecessors, the United States had first to determine what lands were already legally occupied. To do so, Congress sent Commissioners into the newly acquired lands to hold hearings and to make recommendations to the Congress. The actions taken by Congress on these recommendations appear in the *American State Papers,* Public Lands. The thousands of claims to land were organized into classes, and Congress acted on them by class, approving some and disallowing others.

Again, persons who could not document their claims generally lost them, at least at first. Under one U.S. program, however, lands could be claimed by "settlement" rights, that is, by the claimant's showing that he had occupied and improved the land for so many years and that no other person also claimed it. Not more than 640 acres could be claimed by such means. Some who could not show perfected titles from a British or Spanish source could, after all, claim land under settlement rights. Again, Congress was keen to cultivate the loyalty of the settlers, old and new, in the District, which was then the southwesternmost corner of the United States.

Conclusion

Substantive Findings.   Because of the upheavals that accompanied and followed the making of his map, Wilton's portrayal of the Old Natchez District was doomed to obsolesence. Also, because his use of less than the best sources for his base map, his delineation of the region is indicative, rather than definitive, as a guide to the character of the land in his day. Nevertheless, Wilton does portray the fundamental order on the land, despite the Spanish interregnum. Even though many details of the British colonial land administration vanished under the press of events, the *kind* of order that the British established remains to this day. Three mechanisms worked to maintain this basic legal land culture. The first was the initial implantation itself, long recognized by geographers to be very durable. The second mechanism was the Spanish policy of generally continuing the local custom in the District. And the third was the subsequent arrival of American dominion, which had the effect of reestablishing British common law, albeit in its derived form.

Despite any spatial inaccuracies, then, William Wilton did portray in his map of 1774 the establishment of order upon the land.

Residual Questions

1. What was the intended status and intended purpose of the "Reserved" lands located at stream junctures?

2. Did Gov. Peter Chester order the survey of Wilton and perhaps that of Elias Durnford to measure the *mortmain* effect of the mandamus grants?

3. Which of the registered grants belong to persons brought in by holders of madamus grants?

4. Which of the registered grants were re-assignments of land assigned under earlier grants?

Notes

1. Gordon M. Wells, "British Land Grants—William Wilton Map, 1774." *Journal of Mississippi History,* 28 (1966), 152-60.
2. Wells.
3. Margaret Fisher Dalrymple, *The Merchant of Manchac: The Letterbooks of John Fitzpatrick, 1768-1790.* Baton Rouge: LSU Press, 1978, pp. 123 *et passim.*

4. Elias Durnford [Map of the Comite and Amite Rivers], 1771. Colonial Office, Florida, 49, Public Record Office, London.

5. George Gauld, "A Plan of the Coast of Part of West Florida & Louisiana . . . as high up as the River Yazous," 1778.

6. Ph. Pittman, "A Draft of Massiac Lake, Maurepas, part of the River Amitt and the River Ibberville." Copied from Lieut. Ph. Pittman by Wm. Brasiers, [1765].

7. William F. Guste. Re: Trudeau Tract, Section 53, T1S, R4W, Greensburg Land District, West Feliciana Parish, Louisiana. Unpublished Attorney General's opinion, Baton Rouge, August 25, 1978, p. 2.

8. *American State Papers*, 1, p. 609.

"The Remotest Corner":
Natchez on the American Frontier

Morton Rothstein

The draft of a 1799 petition from some Natchez residents to Congress listed various "wants and . . . peculiar circumstances" of settlers in the district, which it called "the most remote corner of the United States."[1] Most of the complaints reflected typical frontier concerns, but the sense of isolation and insecurity pervading this document was unusually strong. It resembles the urgent desperation in Faulkner's portrayal of the mail rider in *Requiem for a Nun*, galloping down the Natchez Trace to bring letters from the distant nation to which the settlement had just been admitted. For almost thirty years before the petition, a mostly English-speaking vanguard had precariously sustained themselves along the solitary bluff, importing slaves to clear land and plant crops on that periphery of the far-flung Atlantic economy. Formidable distances and natural obstacles had separated them from families and friends left behind. By the end of the eighteenth century they still faced many of the same hazards in building a viable economy on the southwestern fringe of the untested new nation. To be sure, the natural resources at hand were rich, and the riverine site held obvious market advantages. But the district still stood where contending ambitions of major nations dangerously collided.[2]

In 1830, a single generation later, they and their children, augmented by a steady flow of migrants from every part of the seaboard, were safely implanted in a bustling town on the main waterway of a rapidly growing nation. Safe and prosperous, with virtually unlimited prospects, Natchez had strong business ties to merchants and traders at both the Atlantic seaboard and overseas in European markets hungry for the district's cotton. The meager cluster of a hundred or so modest houses above the river had flowered into a fabled town of elegant public and private buildings, the embodiment of an already mythic plantation culture. It was a change brought in large measure by the unusually able, energetic businessmen in the front ranks of the town's social order. As much as any group of entrepreneurs in the newly opened Alabama and Mississippi cotton districts, they were also poised eagerly to cash in on the "flush times" that lay ahead.[3]

The district's history began when the British sent a small garrison and handful of settlers to this strategic spot in the 1760s. They did so partly to hold the lands they had just acquired in their victory over France and partly in the hope that they could divert the fur trade from New Orleans, then in Spanish hands, to their own ports. After all, with the possible exception of the cod fisheries, that was the oldest, most reliable business in British North America, drawing on apparently unlimited natural resources and products valuable enough to make the trade risks worthwhile.[4]

To be sure, about fifty years earlier, France had tried on the same spot and for similar reasons to put a fort and a colony among the Natchez Indians, with calamitous results for all concerned. During the ensuing long interval, neither the remnant of that tribe nor the French at New Orleans could reoccupy the place. At the same time, the western European nations, engaged in a global competition for empire, grew more powerful as warriors, more efficient as shippers, more sophisticated as traders. Gradual but fundamental shifts in their culture and ideas, as well as in their economies, had begun to accelerate noticeably by the mid-eighteenth century. Later historians would describe the more rapid pace of technical and economic change as the Industrial Revolution, or as "modernization."[5]

It seems remarkable that the Natchez settlement survived. The British founded several other colonies about the same time in East Florida, closer to lines of supply and to markets at adjoining seaboard colonies, and gave them greater financial and military support. The British dispensed land grants there that were far more generous and more numerous than those at Natchez. They also recruited groups of Italian and Greek peasants to produce silk, wine, and other luxury goods that would fit better into the trading patterns favored by the mercantilist doctrines of the age. Yet all the efforts in East Florida failed miserably. Soon, the British also viewed their West Florida colony as too expensive to hold merely for its questionable strategic benefits. It yielded little else, a problem Spain also faced in neighboring Louisiana. The causes were simple. By the 1770s the continent's fur trade had reached its peak and was beginning to decline. In any case it stayed largely in the hands of a few experienced trading firms such as Panton, Leslie & Company. The only field crops with commercial value, tobacco and indigo (by every account an item exceptionally messy to grow and to process), required the same intensive use of slave labor and even heavier subsidies at Natchez than they did in the Caribbean or on the Atlantic coast.[6]

The handful of adventurers occupying Natchez for British West Florida were also much farther from markets of the Gulf of Mexico and Europe. The river route to the ocean often was closed—or at least threatened with closure—at New Orleans, and the combined water and land route by way of Manchac to Mobile remained prohibitively expensive for bulky farm produce of any kind; return shipments upstream were even more costly. Any merchant therefore confronted large risks in his operations at Natchez, and prices reflected those risks. For years to come newcomers and travelers would agree that the lovely site was also "the most expensive place in the universe."[7]

In their search for marketable products from which to make a living, the district's planters turned to livestock and to the local timber sources. Cutting cypress and oak trees into deals and boards, staves and shingles, kept slaves busy in slack periods and the items almost always found buyers. As late as the 1820s a planter such as the young William Liddell could pay for much of his new land and buildings from the sales of cypress logs. Many settlers in the Natchez area also owned cattle and hogs that roamed the woods, fattening on the mast of the great oaks. On the other hand, there is no record of serious efforts to grow flax or hemp, plants the Spanish then subsidized for farmers in the New Orleans hinterland. Little wonder that trading (and rustling) livestock, along with land jobbing, received so much attention from the district's more enterprising or more desperate residents.[8]

These inauspicious beginnings for Natchez improved little with the coming of the American Revolution. Divided in their loyalties regarding that struggle, but mostly willing to submerge their differences in the common pursuit of economic gain, the district's settlers soon found themselves, like their counterparts in British East Florida, sacrificed to larger imperial considerations. In 1779 troops under a new, energetic Spanish leader at New Orleans recaptured the Floridas and easily swept Natchez into the bag of loot, while the British interest in the gulf region

94

focused on capturing Havana. As a result, Spain held the entire American Gulf Coast as a buffer to protect the richer parts of their empire in Mexico and in the Caribbean. In postwar negotiations they even regained Cuba. The British readily exchanged those bargaining chips for Gibraltar. One might wonder how much a piece of the rock really should have been worth, but we must recall that in 1763 Lord North had worried that the British public would not forgive him, as prime minister, for taking the whole of Canada from France instead of the revenue-producing sugar islands of Guadeloupe and Martinique.[9]

As a "gew gaw" of empire that, like East Florida, had wound up under Spanish rule, Natchez fared much better than most of its settlers expected. Spanish governors tried to strengthen their hold by using land grants to lure settlers from the United States, the one source of numerous, restless people seeking opportunities west of the Atlantic seaboard and north of the Rio Grande. It would take such hardy, energetic people to improve the town's economic base, and the Spanish knew it. To be sure, their grants sometimes overlapped those from the British regime, creating much confusion and, later, much employment for lawyers. But as Americans spilled in ever greater numbers across the mountains, Spain reassessed and altered this policy. It was always a delicate matter for them to govern Natchez, taking much finesse about such decisions as whether to keep subsidizing tobacco and indigo, or to renew the trading privileges at both Natchez or New Orleans of the Philadelphia-based merchants.[10]

Vacillation over such issues might have been expected, and policy shifts came often as the Spanish borderlands began their long, slow retreat. Even the shrewd, decent Gayoso could not, as governor of Natchez, allay the settlers' growing fears and resentments under such circumstances, aggravated as they were by a market crisis that hit the district's planters hard. The cancellation of subsidies merely reinforced the shift in demand due to better supplies suddenly available elsewhere, notably in Asia.[11]

The redrawing of the boundary between Spain and the United States at the 31st parallel that began in 1795 put Natchez in a wholly new economic situation. Its residents not only got full citizenship in the "first new nation," but did so just when cotton was quickly replacing old export crops across much of the South. Friction between planters and merchants (themselves often large-scale holders of land and slaves) remained, however, replicating the typical frontier tensions between creditors and debtors that shaped the district's politics for years.[12]

Yet as part of a nation with more than half a million citizens already living west of the Appalachians, the town benefited from new, vital commercial links with merchants in such frontier river markets as Louisville and Nashville. The leading Natchez traders also drew on credit emanating from counting houses in Philadelphia and in Liverpool.[13]

The new crop and new century brought a short, heady prosperity to the region. The Louisiana Purchase in 1803 gave additional security to commerce and opened new frontier lands across the Mississippi and up the Red River. For the largest planters, diversification in a second major crop, sugar cane, soon proved attractive in areas that lay farther south and west in Louisiana when the cotton boom subsided during embargoes and the War of 1812.[14]

In the long run, however, 1811 was the important year for Natchez and for the entire American frontier. That year saw the defeat of Tecumseh in the Old Northwest and the opening of the Creek War in the Old Southwest, conflicts that broke the effective resistance of native Americans to incursions by whites; it was only a matter of time before the Indians lost their lands, which then accounted for about two-thirds of Mississippi's acreage. In 1811, too, the first steamboat appeared on the Mississippi River, heralding a new era, the start of a transportation revolution crucial to the growth and development of the West. With these events, the major barriers to the full growth of the plantation economy in the lower Mississippi Valley were breached. The Natchez District was becoming fully integrated into both the national and the Atlantic economies. Its isolation ended, it no longer stood at a corner but rather near the center of a more broad-based national economy.[15]

The human dimensions of these sweeping changes can be illustrated by three outstanding men, each representing a different stage in the district's growth. Each earned a prominent place among the Natchez elite; each became a "nabob," as such leaders called themselves.[16] They knew and were related to each other, by blood or marriage, but they played quite different roles.

The first is William Dunbar, a son of the Scottish Enlightment as well as of a British lord. Bernard Bailyn, in his extraordinary work, *Voyagers to the West*, devotes much of a chapter on colonial West Florida to Dunbar, comparing him to Thomas Sutpen, the protagonist of Faulkner's *Absalom, Absalom!*, as an example of rapacious acquisitiveness, but his point seems overdrawn. To be sure, Dunbar on occasion treated his slaves, whose labor built his several plantations, cruelly, but Bailyn concedes that by the prevailing standards of the time "Sir" William was an indulgent master.[17]

He certainly understood the niceties of getting and holding property, whether under the British, the Spanish, or the Americans. The twenty-two-year-old Dunbar arrived in Philadelphia with a batch of London dry goods in 1771, and traded with Indians from a base at Fort Pitt for the next two years, during which time he also acquired a partner and good contacts among merchants in the City of Brotherly Love, then took the long ride downriver to Baton Rouge. After selecting a choice tract of land on a river bank near the British post at Manchac, he registered the title to his grant at Pensacola, then hurried to Jamaica for a cargo of the slaves he needed to launch his plantation enterprise. For the next ten years Dunbar buried himself in the work of building that "agricultural factory," as Bailyn calls it, extracting all the saleable items he could from the land and from its forest cover, experimenting with rice, tobacco, cotton, and some indigo, as well as corn, fruits, and vegetables for home consumption. At first, lumber proved the most profitable. Dunbar put his slaves to work making barrelheads and staves on a large scale for the sugar and molasses of the Caribbean; he once had 100,000 staves piled on his wharf for shipment to the West Indies.[18]

His diary contains no indication that he had any interest in the American Revolution or its outcome, but when the line drawn by the peace treaty of 1783 placed him on the Spanish side, after ten years under British rule, he moved north to within a few miles of English-speaking Natchez and built a new plantation, named, appropriately enough, The Forest, where he spent the rest of his life. He tempered another dozen years under Spanish rule in Natchez with the company of such educated leaders in the Natchez community as Esteban Minor, who was the governor's aide and advisor, and Bernard Lintot. Yet Bailyn sees Dunbar as a man whose basic nature was altered by residing four thousand miles from the culture that had nurtured him. He writes that on the "far periphery of British civilization . . . where ruthless exploitation was a way of life . . . where disorder, violence, and human degradation were commonplace, he had triumphed by successful adaptation. Endlessly enterprising and resourceful . . . he emerged a distinctive new man, a borderland gentleman, a man of property in a raw, half-savage world."[19]

Dunbar's scientific accomplishments gave him a unique position and special leverage within the district's elite. Shortly after moving there,

during the last years of Spanish rule, he served as assistant surveyor for
Gayoso, taking payment for these and other services in land grants that
included several key town lots, among which was much of the landing
stage at Natchez-Under-the-Hill. Some of the land had belonged to the
Spanish government, some to Gayoso himself. Soon after the Americans
took over, Dunbar befriended Governor Sargent, Judge Rodney, and
other new officials, remaining at the center of the town's circle of
"Federalists of the old school" at the same time that he was correspond-
ing with Jefferson about scientific matters. After 1803, when the Red
River became an American waterway at its lower reaches, Dunbar and
his friend Dr. John Sibley not only shared duties as government explorers
and naturalists, but both of them obtained land at Saline Lake northeast
of Natchitoches, where each erected a salt works. For the next few years
Dunbar profited from shipments of that salt, the truly indispensable
frontier commodity, to both Natchez and New Orleans. His land and
cattle, timber and salt, indigo and tobacco gave him a handsome income,
much of which he reinvested in more land and more slaves for his
children. But it was cotton that made him rich. As early as 1797 he wrote
his friend John Ross that "the foundation of a large fortune may be laid
now within this country. . . . Cotton has become the universal crop."[20]

Essential to his success was his ability to tap the credit and services of
merchants based in distant commercial centers. George Green, of
Green, Wainwright & Company, in Liverpool was his major correspon-
dent by 1800 and would be one of the major handlers of Natchez
business well into the 1830s. The business of serving a coterie of the
town's leading planters was important enough to draw Green there
regularly. He often found competitors there, too. George Salkeld, of
Barclay, Salkeld & Company, for example, visited Natchez several times
between 1795 and 1810 to conduct business not only with Dunbar but
with Esteban Minor, Minor's brother John, and with Winthrop Sargent.[21]

In dealing with these merchants and with others involved in his
various interests, Dunbar obtained help in the last decade of his life from
a new son-in-law, Samuel Postlethwaite, the second exemplary figure.
Born into a leading Carlisle, Pennsylvania, family with strong ties to
Philadelphia's business community, he apparently had attained some
success as a merchant in Lexington, Kentucky when he came down the
river for the first time on his own flatboat from Pittsburgh in 1800. The
twenty-eight-year-old bachelor encountered a group of horsemen near
Walnut Hills about to "proceed into the Spanish country 400 m. thro'
diff't nations of savages, for the purpose of catching wild horses," under

one Philip Nolan, and thus saw a Natchez myth in the making. Two days farther south Samuel supped with John B. Scott, Judge Peter Bryan Bruin's son-in-law and a man in the "cotton trade" (with South Carolinian Wade Hampton, probably the South's richest planter, and John C. Nightingale). But it was Natchez that truly impressed Samuel. He sold what remained of his small cargo of flour, bacon, and wood, including the raft on which he traveled, to Abijah Hunt, one of the district's most successful early planters and merchants, for $75, then saw owners of the next boat in the group with which he traveled sell their load on partial credit for $7,000.[22]

He returned for good in 1802, opened a store, and entered the town's civic life by serving as captain of the Natchez Artillery. One of Samuel's business assets was his connection with Thomas & John Clifford, merchants in Philadelphia heavily involved in the New Orleans trade. He explained to them soon after he began trading that he sold "only in a retail way, and on a shameful & injurious long credit," so that he could not handle some of their surplus goods or collect overdue small debts for them. He also explained that "our situation here is really very unpleasant—the Government at N. Orleans seem determined to throw every difficulty in the way of our Trade—The Deposit is yet closed and no prospect of any change." Yet two months later, Postlethwaite had no trouble sending on a cargo of tobacco from Lexington to Liverpool, and within a year, while Spain still occupied New Orleans, he sent several cargoes of cotton to Philadelphia for reshipment to the same British market. By October, 1803, his business was flourishing, and he could report that the imminent surrender of New Orleans would not attract him, as it did many others about to leave Natchez: "I cannot . . . see any great advantage to be derived there without large Capital," he asserted, but did note that the access to the better banking and shipping facilities certain to grow in the Crescent City would help commerce in Natchez.[23]

He found other attractions nearby, and married Ann Dunbar, William's youngest daughter, in 1805. Soon after, Postlethwaite was handling some of an ailing "Sir" William's varied business interests, while investing his own funds in nearby plantations on both sides of the Mississippi. Several other migrants from Carlisle were doing much the same, among them Samuel's brother Henry and a few nieces and cousins. In October, 1810, Samuel set out on an arduous journey, leading several pirogues loaded with trade goods up the Red River, slogging around the Great Raft that blocked that waterway to reach "the Saline" near Natchitoches. He supervised for two weeks the restoration of Dunbar's salt business, left it

99

under a new foreman, and examined the Dunbar livestock herds nearby. He returned with a full load to Natchez just in time to learn that his "much loved, & honored father in law" had died a few days earlier. Dunbar had provided for most of his several children with handsome properties, but his holdings were so complex that it would take years for Samuel, as designated executor of Dunbar's will, to help settle the estate. Control of those assets was very helpful to a man joining the town's inner circle. Evidence of his rising status is found in his involvement in the founding of the Bank of Mississippi, which held a monopoly in the territory and the state until 1830.[24]

More than two years before Dunbar's death, Samuel's nephew Stephen Duncan, the third exemplar, had arrived in Natchez, twenty-one years old and fresh from medical training under Benjamin Rush at the University of Pennsylvania. Almost a half century later Duncan recalled, in a chat with Benjamin L. C. Wailes, that when he first landed at Natchez-Under-the-Hill in 1808 an army officer he knew, pushing off down the river, shouted a warning for him to stay away from one of the taverns. He also recalled that when he began visiting local plantations he could still see the remains of the indigo vats, so recently supplanted by cotton gins.[25]

Duncan began a medical practice and immediately fit into Natchez society. He had several other relatives from the Carlisle and Philadelphia area, including Thomas Butler, of St. Francisville, Louisiana. Duncan joined a Natchez dancing club, where he began a lifelong friendship with Washington Jackson, a merchant originally from Philadelphia who had left a Nashville partnership with his brother and was setting up branches of his own business in Natchez; he had a store and a warehouse, and in 1813 he advertised that the first steam-powered cotton press in the district was at his establishment. Within a few years Jackson also had other branches in New Orleans, in Philadelphia, and in Liverpool, a common arrangement among commercial and banking houses doing business in the "North Atlantic Triangle."[26] Duncan also cherished an early friendship with John Ker, son of the first territorial judge. He, too, was a medical man, and later moved to Louisiana but stayed close to Natchez affairs for decades.

A few years after his arrival, Dr. Duncan married Margaret Ellis, daughter of one of the first settlers in the district. Duncan turned his wife's dowry lands on the Homochitto River into thriving cotton plantations and soon earned enough to increase his holdings, building along with them a solid reputation as one of the shrewdest, most energetic businessmen in Natchez. Still, various afflictions brought doubts along with success. His wife's death, in 1816, left Duncan distraught, and several times over the next few years he considered returning to his family in Pennsylvania. By then he was too involved in the community's life to depart easily, and he also had to admit that he hated the bitter northern winters. A second marriage, to Catherine Bingaman, tied him to such additional members of the business and planter elite as James C. Wilkins and John Linton (partners in the town's leading mercantile house) as well as the colorful Adam L. Bingaman.[27]

Duncan was increasingly concerned about the recurrent visitations of scourges in the region, particularly yellow fever, which had taken his first wife, his uncle Henry Postlethwaite, and many friends. He had long since abandoned his medical practice, keenly aware of the simple fact that doctors then could do little good and much harm to their patients. After a bout of disease racked the Butlers in 1822, Duncan advised Thomas to take his family to "the Northern states, or to the South of France." Duncan admitted that he was himself considering such a move, because the district was "so cursed with disease of every description." He admitted that once "there was no country I wd. prefer to this, but for the last 5 years we have had scarcely anything to speak of half the year, but disease and death," and that he was himself "half-resolved" to live permanently in a "seat near Philadelphia."[28]

Yet by 1825, when Samuel Postlethwaite suddenly died at his mansion, Clifton, and Duncan succeeded his uncle as president of the Bank of Mississippi, the doctor was fully committed to life in Mississippi. His new family was growing; his various investments in sugar lands in the Attakapas region to the southwest and in the cotton lands nearby were flourishing under his astute management; he was the treasurer of a local steamboat company and a silent partner in Andrew Brown's lumber business; and he had earned the respect of the leading citizens. It was in Auburn, the home he purchased from Lyman Harding's heirs, that he and some of those citizens made the plans for enlarging the Trinity Episcopal church. By then he was also helping his sister, Mary Ann Gustine, settle her family in Natchez, including two of her brothers-in-law, and two bright young cousins from Carlisle seeking better career opportunities as lawyers, Duncan and Robert J. Walker.[29]

It was through such family relationships that much of the Natchez District was settled in the early years of the republic. These latecomers could choose several routes for their migrations, and traveled with greater comfort and speed. They arrived in a town with churches, schools, and most of the amenities of the age, all built out of the capital accumulated by the two pioneering generations. It was still a civilization based on a doomed labor system, and there were some premonitions of the ultimte bloody resolution that lay ahead.

In 1830 the town celebrated the opening of former Indian lands in the northern two-thirds of the state, a ceremony that featured a round of toasts by James C. Wilkins, Robert J. Walker, and other notables of the district delighted by the prospective extension of the state's cotton kingdom. Yet soon after that dinner, Stephen Duncan warned that any expansion would bring more blacks to a state where they were already so numerous as "to excite serious apprehensions for our SAFETY." By his count, "in this county (exclusive of the city) we have 4 blacks to one white; a disproportion sufficiently great to make every mother bring her infant more closely to her bosom."[30]

News of the Nat Turner rebellion had arrived in the Natchez District. For better or for worse, the fears it produced would quickly fade, just as did the memory of the many abrupt changes and discontinuities that marked the frontier era in Natchez. It was one of the ironies of the district's history, as it was for the south as a whole, that the new economic boom based on cotton should foster an illusion of permanence, an illusion that was itself the antithesis of frontiers and of the modern industrial age of which this one was so much a part.[31]

Notes

1. Winthrop Sargent Papers, Massachusetts Historical Society, Reel 5, Box 5, draft by Ebenezer Dayton.

2. For a recent work that places the district's early settlement in its broadest perspective, with many helpful maps and diagrams, see Donald W. Meinig, *The Shaping of America: A Geographical Perspective on 500 Years of History*, vol. I, *Atlantic America, 1492–1800* (New Haven: Yale University Press, 1986), 195–203, 281–82, 334–37, 348–70. For a historian's conventional approach, see John Anthony Caruso, *The Southern Frontier* (Indianapolis: Bobbs-Merrill, Co., 1963; On the extent of isolation see D. Clayton James, *Antebellum Natchez* (Baton Rouge: Louisiana State University Press, 1968), 14–30 and Charles S. Sydnor, *A Gentleman of the Old Natchez Region: Benjamin L. C. Wailes* (Durham: Duke University Press, 1938), 6–12. See also the letter from Winthrop Sargent to Timothy Pickering, December 20, 1798, in Dunbar Rowland, comp.

and ed., *The Mississippi Territorial Archives, 1798–1803* (Nashville: Brand Printing Co., 1905), 89–91, in which Sargent laments "our distant and defenseless state."

3. Joseph G. Baldwin, *The Flush Times of Alabama and Mississippi: A Series of Sketches* (New York: D. Appleton & Co., 1853); Joseph Holt Ingraham, *The South-West, By a Yankee* (2 vols.; New York: Harper & Brothers, 1835).

4. John Preston Moore, "Anglo-Spanish Rivalry on the Louisiana Frontier, 1763–68," in John Francis McDermott (ed.), *The Spanish in the Mississippi Valley, 1762–1804* (Urbana: University of Illinois Press, 1974), 72–86. For the broader context of British and Spanish colonial policies and rivalries, see Peggy K. Liss, *Atlantic Empires: The Network of Trade and Revolution, 1713–1826* (Baltimore: The Johns Hopkins University Press, 1982), and the classic work by Arthur P. Whitaker, *The Spanish-American Frontier: 1783–1795* (Lincoln: Bison Books; University of Nebraska Press, 1969).

For an interesting recent study of the role of the fur trade in the entire North American economy, and between the British, French, and Hispanic possessions in the Atlantic, see Fernand Ouellet, "Colonial Economy and International Economy: The Trade of the St. Lawrence River Valley with Spain, Portugal and Their Atlantic Possessions, 1760–1850," in Jacques A. Barbier and Allan J. Kuethe (eds.), *The North American Role in the Spanish Imperial Economy, 1760–1819* (Manchester: Manchester University Press, 1984), 71–110. The classic works on these colonial extractive trades are by Harold A. Innis, *The Cod Fisheries: the History of an International Economy* (Revised edition, Toronto: University of Toronto Press, 1954) and his *The Fur Trade in Canada*, (2nd revised edition; University of Toronto Press, 1956).

5. For an exceptionally trenchant series of commentaries on this shift, see William N. Parker, *Europe, America, and the Wider World: Essays on the Economic History of Western Capitalism*, vol. I, *Europe and the World Economy* (Cambridge: Cambridge University Press, 1984), 141–88.

6. Bernard Bailyn, *Voyagers to The West: A Passage in the Peopling of America on the Eve of the Revolution* (New York: Knopf, 1986), 430–74, 475–88; There is much new light on this firm, its successor, and the region's trade in William S. Coker and Thomas D. Watson, *Indian Traders of the Southeastern Spanish Borderlands: Panton, Leslie & Company and John Forbes & Company, 1783–1847* (Pensacola: University of West Florida Press, 1986). It should be supplemented in terms of legal fall-out involving the heirs of Alexander McGilvray by their 1820s case before the Louisiana Supreme Court, in the Collection of their records, Acct. 106, Docket #1156, Department of Archives and Manuscripts, Earl K. Long Library, University of New Orleans. On the broader context of British policy and its goals, see Dorothy V. Jones, *License for Empire: Colonialism by Treaty in Early America* (Chicago: University of Chicago Press, 1982), 39–45, 140–45, 158–85; William S. Coker, "Spanish Regulation of the Natchez Indigo Industry, 1793–1794: The South's First Antipollution Laws?" *Technology and Culture* 13 (January, 1972), 55–58; Jack D. L. Holmes, "Indigo in Colonial Louisiana and the Floridas," *Louisiana History*, 8 (1967), 329–49.

7. Robert Stark to "My Dear Polly," ca. 1807, in Wilkinson-Stark Family Papers, Historic New Orleans Collection; Lee Soltow, "Oliver Wolcott's Mississippi River Account of 1799," *Southern Studies* 21 (Winter, 1982), 409–32. For a merchant's report on high prices for such provisions as flour, corn, and bacon, explained as due to the "proportionate values of everything else" in Natchez, see J. Weir to William A.

Thompson, February 24, 1803, in Society Collection, Pennsylvania Historical Society, Philadelphia.

8. Summary by William St. John Elliott Liddell of his planting experience, Lhanada, Louisiana, December 15, 1856, in Liddell Family Papers, Louisiana State University. John Hebron Moore, "The Cypress Lumber Industry of the Lower Mississippi Valley During the Colonial Period," *Louisiana History* 24 (Winter, 1983), 25–47. See also the description of this activity in Captain Philip Pittman, *The Present State of the European Settlements on the Mississippi* . . . (facsimile edition, edited and with Introduction and Notes by John Francis McDermott, Memphis State University Press, 1977), especially 23–24, with the indication that "Many of the planters have sawmills, which are worked by the waters of the Mississippi in the time of the floods, and then they are kept going night and day till the waters fall." On the Spanish subsidies, see Brian E. Coutts, "Flax and Hemp in Spanish Louisiana, 1777–1783," *Louisiana History* 26 (Spring, 1985), 129–39. For a study of the problems under the British, see Byrle A. Kynerd, "British West Florida," and Jack D. L. Holmes, "A Spanish Province, 1779–1798," both in Richard A. McLemore (ed.), *A History of Mississippi* (2 vols.; Hattiesburg: University and College Press of Mississippi, 1973), I, 134–57, 158–73. A vivid picture of the restraints on development also emerges from correspondence between Natchez and the nearest British trading posts, in Margaret Fisher Dalrymple (ed.), *The Merchant of Manchac: The Letterbooks of John Fitzpatrick, 1768–1790* (Baton Rouge: Louisiana State University Press, 1978).

9. Cecil Johnson, "Expansion in West Florida, 1770–1779," *Mississippi Valley Historical Review* 20 (March, 1934), 481–96; Jack M. Sosin, *The Revolutionary Frontier, 1763–1783* (New York: Holt, Rinehart and Winston, 1967); Robin F. A. Fabel, "West Florida and British Strategy in the American Revolution" in Samuel Proctor, ed. *Eighteenth Century Florida and the Revolutionary South* (Gainesville: University Presses of Florida, 1978), 49–67. Clarence W. Alvord, *The Mississippi Valley in British Politics* (2 vols.; Cleveland: The Arthur H. Clark Co., 1917), I, 1–5.

10. J. Barton Starr, "'Left as a Gewgaw': The Impact of the American Revolution on British West Florida," in Procter (ed.), *Eighteenth Century Florida*, 14–37; Lawrence Kinnaird, "American Penetration into Spanish Louisiana," in *New Spain and the Anglo-American West: Historical Contributions Presented to Herbert Eugene Bolton*, 2 vols. (Lancaster, Pa.: n. p., 1932), 211–38. For the strong reaction to Spanish rule of the more numerous French settlers at New Orleans and environs, see John Preston Moore, *Revolt in Louisiana: the Spanish Occupation, 1766–1770* (Baton Rouge: Louisiana State University Press, 1976); J. Barton Starr, *Tories, Dons, and Rebels: the American Revolution in British West Florida* (Gainesville: University Presses of Florida, 1976). Robert V. Haynes, *The Natchez District and the American Revolution* (Jackson: University Press of Mississippi, 1976); William S. Coker, "The Bruins and the Formulation of Spanish Immigration Policy in the Old Southwest, 1787–1788," in McDermott, ed. *Spanish in the Mississippi Valley*, 61–71. For an interesting recent discussion of attitudes in the new United States towards the flow of immigration to the West, see Peter S. Onuf, "Liberty, Development, and Union: Visions of the West in the 1780s," *William and Mary Quarterly*, 43 (April 1986), 179–213. Jack D. L. Holmes, *Gayoso: the Life of a Spanish Governor in the Mississippi Valley, 1789–1799* (Baton Rouge: Louisiana State University Press, 1965), gives many details on the problems at Natchez with which the last Spanish commander there had to deal. See also Bruce Tyler, "The Mississippi River Trade, 1784–

1788," *Louisiana History* 12 (1971), 255–62; Carmelo Richard Arena, "Philadelphia-Spanish New Orleans Trade: 1789–1803," (unpublished doctoral dissertation, University of Pennsylvania, 1959); Gilbert C. Din, "War Clouds on the Mississippi: Spain's 1785 Crisis in West Florida," *Florida Historical Quarterly 60* (July, 1981), 51–77. On the methods by which trade on the Mississippi and its tributaries was carried out, see John Amos Johnson, "Pre-Steamboat Navigation on the Lower Mississippi River," (unpublished doctoral dissertation, Louisiana State University, 1963).

11. John G. Clark, *New Orleans, 1718–1812: An Economic History* (Baton Rouge: Louisiana State University Press, 1970), 181–249; Abraham P. Nasatir, *Borderland in Retreat: From Spanish Louisiana to the Far Southwest* (Albuquerque: University of New Mexico Press, 1976).

12. William B. Hamilton, "Politics in the Mississippi Territory," *Huntington Library Quarterly* 11 (May, 1948), 277. For a more detailed discussion see his "American Beginnings in the Old Southwest: The Mississippi Phase," (unpublished doctoral dissertation, Duke University, 1937). For some interesting observations by a contemporary, see Mary L. Thornton, "Letter from David Ker to John Steele, *The Journal of Mississippi History* 25 (April 1963), 135–38. In this report, written in 1801, Ker noted that "this country has had for three or four years an unexampled increase of wealth. The cotton planters were then in debt from former speculation about raising Tobacco & Indigo they are now generally affluent & adding yearly to their gains. An industrious planter clears the price of a negro in year from his labour."

13. Arthur P. Whitaker, *The Mississippi Question, 1795–1803: A Study in Trade, Politics, and Diplomacy* (New York: D. Appleton-Century, 1934), 63–97; Harriet Simpson Arnow, *Flowering of the Cumberland* (New York: Macmillan Co., 1963), 86, 102, 342–49, 379–80. For the early territorial period in general, see Richard A. and Nannie P. McLemore, "The Birth of Mississippi," *The Journal of Mississippi History* 29 (November, 1967), 255–69 and Robert V. Haynes, "Formation of the Territory" in McLemore, ed., *A History of Mississippi*, I, 174–216.

14. For early acquisitions of land grants and investments by Natchez citizens, see Robert Dabney Calhoun, "A History of Concordia Parish Louisiana," *Louisiana Historical Quarterly*, 15 (July, 1932), 428–626; On settlers to the south of Mississippi in the "Florida Parishes," see Prentiss B. Carter, "The History of Washington Parish, Louisiana, as Compiled from the Records and Traditions," *Louisiana Historical Quarterly*, 14 (January, 1931), 44–59. On the general trading conditions, see John G. Clark, *New Orleans*, 275–359, and Francis S. Philbrick, *The Rise of the West, 1754–1830* (The New American Nations Series; New York: Harper & Row, 1965), 210–33.

15. An excellent recent survey of native Americans in the southern United States is J. Leitch Wright, Jr., *The Only Land They Knew: The Tragic Story of the American Indians in the Old South* (New York: Free Press, 1981). On the military history of the Creek War and its wider connections, see Frank L. Owsley, Jr., *Struggle for the Gulf Borderlands: The Creek War and the Battle of New Orleans, 1812–1815* (Gainesville: University Presses of Florida, 1981). On the treatment of Indian nations in Mississippi see Martin Abbott, "Indian Policy and Management in the Mississippi Territory, 1798–1817," *The Journal of Mississippi History* 14 (July, 1952), 153–69; Arthur H. DeRosier, Jr., "The Removal of the Choctaw Indians from Mississippi," (unpublished doctoral dissertation, University of South Carolina, 1959); Charles H. Schoenleber, "Mississippi and the Removal of the Choctaw and Chickasaw Indians, 1817–1832," (unpublished

master's thesis, University of Wisconsin-Milwaukee, 1976); and Daniel H. Usner, "American Indians on the Cotton Frontier: Changing Economic Relations with Citizens and Slaves in the Mississippi Territory," *The Journal of American History,* 72 (September, 1985), 297–317. On the consequences of forcing Indian tribes to accept a land allotment system that was certain to destroy their cohesion, see Mary E. Young: *Redskins, Ruffleshirts, and Rednecks: Indian Allotments in Alabama and Mississippi, 1830–1860* (Norman: University of Oklahoma Press, 1961). The classic study of river commerce is Louis C. Hunter, *Steamboats on the Western Rivers* (Cambridge: Harvard University Press, 1949), 12–51, 326–27.

16. On the origins of the term and its usage in the district, see my article, "The Changing Social Networks and Investment Behavior of a Slaveholding Elite in the Ante-Bellum South: Some Natchez 'Nabobs,' 1800–1860," in Sidney M. Greenfield, *et al.*, (eds.), *Entrepreneurs in Cultural Context* (Albuquerque: University of New Mexico Press, 1979), 65–84. See also, Thomas H. Williams to White Turpin, Jan. 12, 1822 from Washington, D.C., with his remark that "we live better than Nabobs," obviously a common reference to luxury. Benjamin L. C. Wailes Papers, Box 1, Z 76, Mississippi Dept. of Archives and History, Jackson.

17. Bailyn, *Voyagers*, 488–92. For a different view of this figure, see James R. Dungan, "'Sir' William Dunbar of Natchez: Planter, Explorer, and Scientist, 1792–1810," *Journal of Mississippi History* 23 (October, 1961), 211–28.

18. Bailyn, *Voyagers*, 490.

19. *Ibid*, 492. For the circle of friends, see William B. Hamilton, *Anglo-American Law on the Frontier: Thomas Rodney & His Territorial Cases* (Durham, N.C.: Duke University Press, 1953), 85–88, and Jack D. L. Holmes, "Stephen Minor: Natchez Pioneer," *Journal of Mississippi History* 42 (February, 1980), 17–26.

20. On Dunbar's land claims, see *American State Papers, Public Lands*, I (1834), 170–80, Jan. 26, 1804, and *Plan of Settlements Near the Natches*, particularly Mr. Wm. Dunbar's, recd. from C. Ross, Aug. 1803, American Philosophical Society, Philadelphia, a map showing several of the claims just above the 31st parallel. There are also several maps of land grants under the Spanish regime showing various claims by Dunbar and his son Robert in the Natchez-Bouligny Papers, Historic New Orleans Collection. For the letter to his partner, see Eron Rowland (ed.), *Life, Letters and Papers of William Dunbar of Elgin, Morayshire, Scotland, and Natchez, Mississippi: Pioneer Scientist of the Southern United States* (Jackson: National Society of Colonial Dames, 1930), Letter of August, 1797. On Dr. Sibley, see G. P. Whittington, "Dr. John Sibley of Natchitoches, 1757–1837," *Louisiana Historical Quarterly* 10 (October, 1927), 467–73 and Julia K. Garrett, "Doctor John Sibley and the Louisiana-Texas Frontier, 1803–1814," *Southwest Historical Quarterly* 45 (January, 1942), 286–382 and 46 (January, 1943), 272–277. On the salt trade in general, see Yvonne Phillips, "Salt Production and Trade in North Louisiana Before 1870," *Louisiana Studies* (Summer, 1962), 28–46.

21. The Minor Family Papers, Louisiana State University, contain several letters to Bernard Lintot, Manchac, from Salkeld from 1779 on, involving trade with Natchez, and the Minor family papers, University of North Carolina, contain about ten letters dated between 1814 and 1822 from both Barclay & Salkeld and George Green & Co., Liverpool to John Minor, seeking to re-establish direct trade after the War of 1812. Salkeld paid a tax in 1812, according to the Natchez rolls, on a holding of 2026 acres and 82 slaves, presumably the result of a foreclosure. See also, James Hipkins *v.* George

Salkeld, Docket #449, Supreme Court of Louisiana Collection, Department of Archives and Manuscripts, Earl K. Long Library, University of New Orleans.

22. In addition to the brief sketch and letters by and about Postlethwaite in the *Life, Letters and Papers of William Dunbar,* see William D. McCain, (ed.), Samuel Postlethwaite, "Journal of a Voyage from Louisville to Natchez—1800," *Missouri Historical Society Bulletin* 7 (April, 1951), 312–29 and the obituary in *The Natchez Ariel,* November, 7, 1825. On Bruin, see William S. Coker, "Colonel Peter Bryan Bruin, Virginia, Spanish West Florida, and Louisiana Planter," in R. Alton Lee (ed.), *Agricultural Legacies: Essays in Honor of Gilbert C. Fite* (Vermillion, S.D.: University of South Dakota Press, 1986), 105–17. On Hampton's speculations in Natchez District lands, see Ronald E. Bridwell, "The South's Wealthiest Planter: Wade Hampton I of South Carolina, 1754–1835" (unpublished doctoral dissertation, University of South Carolina, 1980) Chapters 7 and 11.

23. S. Postlethwait [*sic*], December 8, 1802, October 20, 1803, to Messrs. Thomas & John Clifford, in Clifford Papers, Pemberton Collection, Pennsylvania Historical Society, Philadelphia.

24. The three travel diaries of his trips up the Red River are in the Postlethwaite Papers, Huntington Library, San Marino, California. I am preparing an article that will transcribe much of this material. For the Great Raft and its later removal, see Edith McCall, *Conquering the Rivers: Henry Miller Shreve and the Navigation of America's Inland Waterways* (Baton Rouge: Louisiana State University Press, 1984), 196–211. On the early history of the Bank, see Robert C. Weems, Jr., "Mississippi's First Banking System," *Journal of Mississippi History* 29 (November, 1967), 386–408. On the house that Postlethwaite built, see Samuel Wilson, Jr., "Clifton—An Ill-Fated Natchez Mansion," *Journal of Mississippi History* 46 (August, 1984), 179–89.

25. Sydnor, *Benjamin L. C. Wailes,* 46; Wailes Diaries, No. 7, p. 3, in Wailes Papers, Duke University; for a fairly reliable genealogical study of Duncan's family, see Katherine Duncan Smith (comp.), *The Story of Thomas Duncan and His Six Sons* (New York: Tobias A. Wright, 1928), 41–49. Duncan and many of his relations at Carlisle, Pa., who later migrated to Natchez attended Dickinson College and received a quite rigorous education for the time. See George L. Reed (ed.), *Alumni Record Dickinson College,* (Carlisle, Pa., 1905), 46–57; Charles C. Sellers, *Dickinson College: A History* (Middletown, Conn.: Wesleyan University Press, 1973).

26. Pierce Butler, *The Unhurried Years: Memories of the Old Natchez Region* (Baton Rouge: Louisiana State University Press, 1948), 7–8, 26–27; Jackson and his brother James were in business at Nashville in Oct., 1804, when Court House Records, Minute Book D, 34–49, indicate they were "attaching" seven bales of cotton; in Nov., 1806, they bought a cotton gin. James Jackson left for Alabama some time later; Washington was taken into partnership with Kirkman & Erwin in 1814, and in 1821 was doing a commission business in Philadelphia. I am indebted to my friend, Prof. Anita Goodstein of the University of the South for this information. For the notice that Jackson "will have a first rate iron screw press set up at Natchez . . . for the purpose of re-pressing cotton for the public" see *Mississippi Republican,* Natchez, February 2, 1814. According to the Directory of Philadelphia, 1832–1837, Washington Jackson was a prominent iron commission merchant in the firm of Jackson & Riddle, a director of the Beaver Meadow Railroad & Coal Co., of the Atlantic Insurance Co., and a candidate in 1838 for selectman on the Philadelphia "fed" ticket. By then he had a branch in Liverpool known

as Jackson, Todd & Co. On Butler, married to a sister of Margaret Ellis Duncan and whose family remained close to Stephen for many years, see Emma Louise M. Dawes, "Judge Thomas Butler of Louisiana: A Biographical Study of an Ante-Bellum Jurist and Planter," (M.A. thesis, Louisiana State University, 1953).

27. Duncan's daughter, Sarah Jane, later married into another prominent Pennsylvania family, and her husband founded a town in the western part of the state with much of his wife's inheritance, and Duncan's later support. Nicholas B. Wainwright, *The Irvine Story* (Philadelphia: Historical Society of Pennsylvania, 1964).

28. S. Duncan to Thomas Butler, September 29, 1822, in Butler Papers, Louisiana State University; Lucie Robertson Bridgforth, "Medicine in Antebellum Mississippi," *Journal of Mississippi History* 40 (May, 1984), 82–107.

29. Robert C. Weems, "The Makers of the Bank of Mississippi," *Journal of Mississippi History* 15 (July, 1953), 137–54; S. Duncan to Thomas Butler, December 15, 1827, in Butler Family Papers, Louisiana State University, which is signed "Stephen Duncan, Treasurer of the 'Steam Boat Walk in the Water'". On his role in the Trinity Church, see Trinity Episcopal Church Records, Mississippi Department of Archives and History, Jackson. For an interesting new analysis of Auburn and other buildings in the Natchez District, see Robert J. Kapsch, "The Use of Numerical Taxonomy in the Study of Historical Buildings in the Natchez, Mississippi, Area" (unpublished doctoral dissertation [Engineering and Architecture], Catholic University of America, Washington, D.C., 1982).

30. S. Duncan to Josiah S. Johnston, Washington, D.C. [Senator from Louisiana] October 11, 1831, in the J. S. Johnston Papers, Pennsylvania Historical Society. One week earlier, Duncan had written to Thomas Butler, "I dont credit the story of the extension of the Virginia insurrection, tho' I have great apprehension that we will one day have our throats cut in this county. We have here 5 blacks to one white, and within 4 hours march of Natchez there are 2200 able bodied male slaves. It behooves us to be vigilant—but SILENT." Robert J. Walker's speech was printed in *Public Dinner of Adams County Citizens, October 10, 1830*. On the fate of the Choctaw Nation before and after removal, see Richard White, *The Roots of Dependency: Subsistence, Environment, and Social Change Among the Choctaws, Pawnees, and Navajos* (Lincoln: University of Nebraska Press, 1983).

31. The now classic statement about discontinuities and basic changes in the history of the South is C. Vann Woodward, "The Irony of Southern History," in his *The Burden of Southern History* (Baton Rouge: Louisiana State University Press, 1960).

The Aesthetics of Everyday Life in Old Natchez

Estill Curtis Pennington

Observation of any particular aspect of antebellum southern material culture requires some reflection on developments in the methodology employed to evaluate extant objects in their proper context. It would seem an over-riding preoccupation with the issues of Southern political and economic history have made it difficult to examine the very *things* of the past with any degree of objectivity. What we really want to know about a people is how they lived, and not only how they lived, but how the world in which they lived was appointed, or, if you will, furnished, and the flavor and color of their lives. Do we imagine that events unfold in assembly rooms, or outdoors amidst large public spaces, surrounded by civic architecture, or in private spaces decreed by taste? If we could be diverted for a moment from the events at hand, would we be distracted by the way in which the room was painted, or what style furniture it contained, how the silver was placed, and whether there were any pictures?

In the South the serious questions of material culture, by and large, have been left to the antiquarians. The importance of objects to full historical study has been somewhat clouded by the seemingly elite aspects of extancy. If a mere object has survived the passage of time, it will very likely have an association with a particular family or individual, and the historical associations of biography almost always lead to the "fine old family" dilemma of southern studies.

The penchant for heirlooms and their connoisseurship is inextricably tied up with the crises and resolution of southern history. If history is indeed dialectical, and if we are faced with simple crossroads, then at the fork of southern art history we are led by the one road to the ecstatic apologies of plantation romance and, by the other, to the severity of economic realities. On the one hand there are those objects, made on site, which reflect both the taste and the materials of the locale, and on the other hand those things that were imported, bringing with them the taste of the area from which they came. The indigenous and the imported, then, are dual partners in the dialectic of southern material culture, for they encompass the making of things and their consumption.

The antiquarian is concerned with the mere survival of an object, its age, and limited historical associations. The art historian is more interested in the formal aspects of design, medium, and style. The most pressing issue that the southern art historian faces is also the most subliminal. As long as the serious preoccupation with slavery is the critical shaping factor of antebellum history and culture, then the material culture of the South will suffer grave neglect.

Slavery was an odious and extraordinarily unfortunate system, but only the most naïve historian will claim that it was more or less odious than any other form of human manumission in the history of the planet. There have been, and are currently, thoughtful historians who have blended the issue into the larger fabric of the time in order to assess its impact upon the entire culture and the lives of the people.

One such writer from the past is Ulrich Bonnell Phillips. His work, *Life and Labor in the Old South*, is an important methodological beacon for the art historian as well as for the cultural historian. In this work he traces the migration of the southern settlers, their trade routes and patterns, and the demands of their labor system. Perhaps the most lasting contribution of the volume is the assessment of plantation housing built by the labor system at hand. History is best served by an acceptance of complexity and contradiction, and in summing up slavery Phillips observes that "The slave regime was a curious blend of force and concession, of arbitrary disposal by the master and self-direction by the slave, of tyranny and benevolence, of antipathy and affection."[1]

Phillips' observations are in a sense dated. For the purposes of understanding southern history, the most important recent writer is the historian Eugene G. Genovese. In his prize-winning volume, *Roll, Jordan, Roll: The World the Slaves Made*, he approaches the slave culture in terms of paternalism and the class struggle. In a highly perceptive remark he characterizes the slave issue as "not merely one more manifestation of some abstraction called racist society. Its history was essentially determined by particular relationships of class power in racial form."[2]

Through his study of race relations of the Old South, Genovese has moved away from the simple didacticism of right and wrong toward a more humanistic dialectic. Assessing antebellum southerners in a book review for the *New York Times*, Genovese wrote that they "qualified, by any reasonable standard, as good and decent people who tried to live decently with their slaves. They were doomed to fail, for their relations with their slaves rested on injustice and violence, and therein lay the tragedy that has made them, individually and as a class, the most arresting of Americans."[3]

These comments are not to divert us from the matter at hand, which is aesthetics. But aesthetics is the study of taste, and taste is borne upon the backs of those who make, for those who consume, and arrange and tidy, for those who appoint. Indeed, slavery is the major consideration in southern material culture studies. To liberate the actual life of the Old South from its lethal mythologizing, to healthy academic scrutiny, one must grapple with slavery as the labor system. Southern art history is still standing outside the door, awaiting integration into the national art historical view. The door will remain shut as long as moonlight and magnolias continue to fall upon our things, and as long as we see them as some remnant to cling to in the face of modernist blasts.

As much as in any other area of the Southland, slavery increasingly became an issue in pre-1830 Natchez. Natchez was a slave trade center. The Natchez papers are full of advertisements for runaway slaves, pitched in great cruelty; individuals were frequently identified by their scars or physical impairments of speech or form. It is all an ugly business, a sad and dreary backdrop to a lively and colorful society living by the river.

Because Natchez was a major trading center and urban source for commodities, slavery was not as extensive in the city as in the county. In the pre-1830 phase of Natchez life, slaves accounted for little more than one-fourth the total population. Charles Sydnor, in his *Slavery in Mississippi*, has pointed out that "a number of Mississippi slaves, neither domestic servants nor agricultural laborers, were commonly spoken of as 'town slaves.'"[4] The tasks they performed were undoubtedly part of the enormous volume of trade being conducted in Natchez with increasing density from the opening of the Baton Rouge road to the utilization of the Natchez Trace as a major conduit of commodity exchange with the upper South after 1801.

By 1800 a contemporary writer could speak of Natchez as "the center of trade for the Western Country."[5] In 1800 Ben Morgan could write home to his kinsman David that Natchez "contains 100 homes and upward, inhabited principally by the storekeepers. . . ." There were also numerous tradesmen who were "in great demand and I can safely say they can earn three times the sum of money in the same length of time here that they can in Pennsylvania."[6]

There were several large stores selling goods from various sources. In the *Mississippi Herald and Natchez Gazette* for October 16, 1807, D. D. Elliot & Company advertised dry goods, shoes, and "a quantity of Cherry Tree Furniture consisting of sideboards, dining tables, bureaus, etc." In the *Mississippi Republican and Literary Register* of August 6, 1818, Thomas Bell announces that he has "laid in at the most reduced prices in Philadelphia sheetings, Super furniture, plates, and other dry goods. . . ." In the same issue, Moyes and Spencer announce the arrival of goods from New Orleans, and the bookseller John Menefee advertises a new stock of books received from New York, including works by that daring rascal Lord Byron.

One of the most important discoveries in a newspaper advertisement makes it possible to define the colors available for home decoration. In the *Mississippi Republican* for September 24, 1818, William E. Lehman announces the arrival of dry paints, or pigments, which could be bound with linseed oil and turpentine: Chinese Vermillian [*sic*], yellow ochre, spruce ochre, stone ochre, whiting, Spanish brown, King's yellow, Dutch pink, rose pink, umber and Redhead are among them.

The entire issue of style and taste is centered upon point of origin, for prevailing high styles and tastes dictated by merchants outside the Natchez region were helping to shape the tastes of the area itself. Upriver from New Orleans came the more international style of the Caribbean basin, styles derived from trade with Spain and France. Certainly the early architecture of Natchez reflects both the climatic concerns of a steamy, humid region and the styles of Caribbean architecture popular in New Orleans. In the furnishings of these houses a stylish French taste, especially for furniture and porcelains, characterized the area right up until the time of the Civil War.

However, in the decade prior to statehood in 1817, the prevailing taste in Natchez was the federalism of the Union cast into great form by Philadelphia craftsmen and given distinct regional flavor by Kentuckians. After Winthrop Sargent became territorial governor in 1798, federalism grew in popularity, as witnessed by increasing accounts of

Washington and Jefferson in the newspapers, and by the importation of goods from Philadelphia. The spare neoclassicism of the federal period would linger long in Natchez, not only in the furnishings of homes, but in the manufacture of silver and in portrait styles.

The central Kentucky plateau was well established as a cultural center by 1788, and the first libraries, colleges, and theaters west of the Alleghenies were located there. Throughout the period following the opening of the territory in 1798, Kentuckians streamed into the Natchez region, bringing their taste and style with them.

For example, when Samuel and Jane Cook Davis came from Fairfield, Kentucky, to Woodville in 1811, they brought along many of their Kentucky furnishings, including a press, or cupboard, of Kentucky cherry, that can be seen 177 years later at Rosemont, their Woodville plantation. Their son, Joseph Emory Davis, was an important trend-setter in the period, as was another Kentuckian, Edward Turner. It was this group of Kentucky settlers who helped to write Mississippi's laws, create a state government, and build important homes and libraries. Curiously enough, genealogy proves a proper handmaiden to art history in these studies. A family's migratory pattern and its extended connections are often the best index of the accumulation of objects that permit an ex post facto statement of taste.

However, Kentucky contributed more than a genteel drawing-room setting to the color of Old Natchez life. Kentucky was the source of tobacco, whiskey, and hemp. The role of the Kentucky flatboatman on the river, and in Natchez-Under-the-Hill, was to swagger, drink excessively, carouse, and bellow out far-fetched tales in the flat drawling tones of the Appalachians. Alexander Wilson, a stalwart traveler in 1810, remarked in a letter that he "arrived [in Natchez] having overcome every obstacle, alone, and without being acquainted with the country, and what surprised the boatmen more, without whiskey."[7]

The consumption of whiskey was not the only occupation in Natchez-Under-the-Hill. There were numerous brothels, gaming houses, and inns where the jolly flatboatmen would put up after their long and treacherous journey down the mighty river. Often several hundred Kentucky keel-boats would be tied up at the docks, bobbing in unison, teeming with life. One popular inn was called The Kentucky and must have resembled the scene described by Wilson, who found his "present situation, a noisy tavern, crowded in every corner, even in the room where I write, with the sons of riot and dissipation," who prevented him "from enlarging on particulars."

Traipsing on the Natchez Trace rivaled rampaging on the river. Highwaymen like Joseph Thompson Hare abounded. These men would listen to the drunken boastings of profit-laden travelers at King's Tavern and then waylay them outside town, relieving them of their booty. Guilt-stricken, Hare claimed to have had a vision of a white horse appearing on the Trace at midnight, symbolizing Christ appealing to him to stop his sins. The vision was unsettling and he was forced to spend the night with a local lady of comfort, but his sins continued until he was hanged in 1818.[8]

Up on the bluff the antics of the river folk were viewed with concern, dismay, and disdain. One of the principal concerns faced by the "pillared folk," as they were known, was the climate and the general state of health. Andrew Marschalk created quite a stir in 1818 when he questioned the healthiness of Natchez as a refuge from the yellow fever scares in New Orleans. The controversy raged on for several issues of the competing newspapers, with the eventual conclusion that Natchez was safe, if for no other reason than its distance from New Orleans.

The climate often disconcerted the northern traveler. Ben Morgan found "the lowness of the river and the excessive heat of the weather made us sometimes think we would have been more comfortable in Morgantown or even in Philadelphia." He continued by outlining the various diseases, "principally fever and ague and yielding quickly to medicine sooner than with us. Indeed by temperance, keeping out the night air, avoiding getting wet and living a few miles from the river nearly the same state of health can be enjoyed as to the northward,"[9] by which he surely meant Pennsylvania and not Vicksburg or Rodney.

The state of health can only have been rivaled by the state of the streets, which, according to one account in 1818, "were not paved, nor have they even the convenience of a paved sidewalk, consequently in wet weather it must be disagreeable walking."[10] But matters are often relative, and James Weir felt that Natchez was "or the inhabitants of the town are, as much given to luxury and dissipation as any place in America."[11]

While Catholicism was in place, Protestantism apparently was not the strongly held spiritual solution of a populace preoccupied with health and the doings of the groundlings below the hill. In October of 1811 the Western Conference of the Methodist Episcopal Church decided to send the Reverend John Johnson of South Carolina to the Natchez circuit. His report reads more like a city directory of a mercantile district than an ecclesiastical assessment of a future flock. After listing several stores, taverns, cabinetmakers, and warehouses, he concludes, "The people in general are very rich, very proud and very polite . . . exceeding all others on compliments . . . but little humility, little religion and little piety."[12]

The absence of piety also accounts for the absence of an actual place of worship. The Reverend Daniel Smith, a Presbyterian minister arriving from Massachusetts in 1815, reports that "in the city of Natchez there has never been an organized protestant church of any denomination. There are a few pious Methodists, Baptists and Presbyterians, but heretofore there were never a sufficient number of either to warrant the formation of a church." He found Natchez to be "deplorably destitute of the means of grace," but possessed of a $400 pulpit. Smith set about creating a public place of worship, Natchez' first Presbyterian meetinghouse, erected in 1815. While these efforts were successful, he only lamented that "the habit of attending public worship was wanting; and it was apprehended that most of the seats would for a long time remain unoccupied."[13]

But Natchez could not withstand the wave of fundamental piety sweeping the country and soon, according to Smith, it "became fashionable to go to church." Such piety is a staple of many of the obituaries that appear in the newspapers of the times. Mrs. Mary B. Holliday, the wife of John Holliday, Esq., was mourned, for "the feature which shone most conspicuously in her character was vital, practical, piety."[14]

Against this backdrop of the sacred and the profane, the spoons and chairs and portraits of old Natchez were laid or stood or hung. The most substantial body of the decorative arts of antebellum material southern culture falls into three important categories: silver, furniture, and portraiture. Silver, being a precious metal with a significant market value, has long been the most seriously studied object of the Old South. Furniture is a more clouded issue, due to the absence of records and the confusion about the source of the object or the site of its manufacture. Portraiture is possessed of the same deep associational values as silver, but in the absence of a strong market has fallen prey to the pitfalls of mistaken mythology and antiquarianism.

There has been very important work done on early Natchez silver by H. Parrott Bacot and Bethany Lambdin.[15] In examining the works of the Natchez silversmiths, these historians have made us aware of three methodological concerns: how these things were made, what shape they took, and what style they affected. Among Natchez silversmiths in the period, Thomas Chester Coit and Emile Profilet are especially notable for the quality of their work and the number of extant examples.

Spoons are the most common surviving pieces of silver, for sociological and practical reasons: such forks as there might have been, for example, were subject to tine breakage and were doubtless often pitched back into the smelter pot. Spoons appear in the literature as the most frequent wedding gift and, next to bed coverings and quilts, the most frequently inventoried item in wills. Most of these spoons seem to have been made by cutting sheets of silver into the requisite forms and joining basin and handle. The most common style of spoon in antebellum culture was the *fiddle thread* or *fiddle back* spoon, so called because of its resemblance to the shape of a fiddle. These spoons had pointed basins, sometimes sharply defined with a raised tip or more gently rounded off. Since spoons were placed basin down on the table, their backs were decorated, a fact which accounts for the raised fiddle pattern on so many of the Natchez spoons of Coit, Robert Houghton, and John S. Miller. There survive as well examples of various ladles and serving pieces, all rendered in the same spare neoclassical style as their companion spoons. The simplicity and the patina of these pieces are most appealing. Although not in any sense a part of a prevailing high style, they may be regarded as interpretative manufactures by local craftsmen.

The source for silver used in crafting these spoons is a subject for disinterested speculation. In Kentucky the prevailing myth is that families accumulated silver coins for the manufacture of their silver, and indeed at least one Kentucky piece has survived, attributed to Profilet, which is actually a stamped coin. In a frontier culture, bartering was a principal means of commodity exchange, since coinage was somewhat limited, and prosperous families in Natchez also may well have converted an enviable specie into a functional object—especially in the absence of banks. It is also possible that they simply bought sheets of silver for manufacture. Many of the Natchez silversmiths who appear in the directories and newspaper advertisements list themselves as merchants for a variety of wares, including watches, tea sets, and clocks, and it does not seem unlikely that they also imported sheets of thinly rolled silver, composites of 900 parts silver and 100 parts copper.

Near 1830, there began to arrive in Natchez a series of itinerant portrait painters who brought the fine arts to the area. Exactly when the first itinerant artist appeared in Natchez is unknown, but it could have been William Edward West, a Kentucky painter with close family ties to the Turners.[16] He is reported to have visited Judge Turner in 1802 while on a flatboat trip down the Mississippi River with the Bourbon County,

Fig. 1. Catherine Surget Bin-
gaman
Oil painting by William Edward West,
The Art Collection, Tulane University
(Linton-Surget Collection) bequest of
Mrs. Eustace Surget and gift of Mrs.
C. B. Surget. Photograph courtesy of
the National Portrait Gallery, Smithso-
nian Institution

Kentucky, merchant Abram Spears. It is possible that a fourteen-year-old boy made this trip in 1802, but whether he took any likeness, to use the language of the time, is doubtful, and no objects from that period survive.

West is a presence in Natchez throughout the decade 1810–1819; he had come upriver to Natchez in 1817 to escape yellow fever in New Orleans. H. A. Huntington placed a notice in the *Natchez Intelligencer* for February 5, 1817, offering for sale a painting, a copy of Raphael's *Madonna and Child* by West, whom Huntington described as "well known in this city and its vicinity." Several portraits by West survive from this most active period in Natchez.

West had received, if not instruction, then at least an apprenticeship of sorts from Thomas Sully, with whom he worked in Philadelphia intermittently between 1810 and 1815. It was from Sully that West appropriated the compositional technique of placing one hand on the bottom flat range of the picture plane, and stretching the figure out in an attenuated manner up the vertical plane. The portraits of Catherine Surget Bingaman (fig. 1), Sarah Buckholtz Richards, and Maria Clarissa Vidal, all have this quality. In this mode West was really avant-garde, functioning in a role familiar to the itinerant painter, that of a messenger

117

of taste. The empire waistlines and vivid coloration of these works would have been in the forefront of portrait taste in New York and Philadelphia. West also worked in the older neoclassical style of Gilbert Stuart, and several works of this type survive as well. Of these, perhaps none is more notable than the portrait of Joseph Emory Davis, the elder brother of Jefferson. There is a probing quality to this work and a grave neoclassical elegance. The muted background, vivid jabot, and deep eyes, combine to make it a masterpiece of minimal restraint.

Portraiture is one of the deepest forms of material culture, for it combines the art-historical concerns of style with the social history of the subject. West's sitters in this period are all representative of broad middle-class taste in Natchez, and he recorded his observations of them not only on canvas but also in his lively journals and letters. The Richardses, for example, are known to have kept an ample wine cellar and to have entertained frequently. The Bingamans were so amusing that West wrote to his sister, "I could go on talking about them forever." He especially admired the Dunbars' dairy and farm for their cleanliness and efficiency. When Maria Clarissa Vidal married Samuel Davis, she was ferried across the river from Louisiana on a barge hung with silks, and she left in a carriage for an elaborate honeymoon in Philadelphia.[17]

Although West departed for Italy in 1819, there were already two other Kentuckians working in Natchez. One, Matthew Harris Jouett, was a student of Gilbert Stuart, in Boston. Jouett was a veteran of the War of 1812. During that conflict he was a paymaster with the Twentieth Regiment of the United States Infantry, and in this role lost some $6,000 in pay vouchers. To make good this debt he embarked upon what could be the profitable business of painting portraits, working in Natchez during the winter seasons. He painted several notable nabobs. Among his best work is a portrait of the little Smith boys, crisp and clear, and very romantically colored (fig. 2).

One letter from February, 1823, tells that Jouett found Natchez a profitable and interesting location for his trade. He had landed at Natchez-Under-the-Hill and "walked up the big hill." Always distracted by the conversation around him, he immediately began to take stock of local problems: "This bustle and apparent commercial activity the people are [conducting] under the most insurmountable load of debt and what adds to the calamity is the low price of cotton. Notwithstanding all this my prospects are fine—had I time I think I could make my visit here a profitable one."[18] Jouett is alluding to the ebb and flow of the cotton

Fig. 2. The Little Smith Boys
Oil painting by Matthew Harris Jouett
Courtesy of Bazile R. Lanneau

market, which before the establishment of the Planter's Bank in 1830 was gravely affected by the vagaries of the international market and the availability of ready cash for Natchez cotton brokers like John Richards, far from their source of capital in Liverpool. Jouett's death at an early age in 1827 ended his travels to Natchez, but he remains a well-known figure.

The third of the Kentuckians to work in Natchez was Joseph Henry Bush. Bush appeared in Natchez in 1818 after a period of work in Kentucky and a time of study with Thomas Sully in Philadelphia. Bush repeated many of the patterns of the Kentucky–Mississippi itinerancy and the styles employed by the common tendencies of the Kentucky portrait school. Bush's best work in Natchez was accomplished after 1830, when he painted such works as the Chotard boys (fig. 3). His unique compositional device of stacking three figures in an interdependent manner on the picture plane separates him from his more federalist fellow Kentuckians.

The only other portraitist known to have worked in the Natchez area prior to 1830 was C. R. Parker, who is thought to have painted silversmith Emile Profilet's portrait in 1830. Parker is an almost legendary figure, for he was the most truly itinerant artist in the Deep South before

Fig. 3. The Chotard Brothers
Oil painting by Joseph Henry Bush
Courtesy of Richard D. Chotard

the war. He is known to have worked in every state from Georgia to Louisiana. So static and repetitive is his work that he is the best candidate for the "headless body" theory of portraiture. Many believe that portrait bodies were carried about on horseback and the face applied at the time of the sitting. This is highly unlikely, due to the marketability of headless bodies, and to the awkwardness of carrying rolled canvas with freshly painted images.

Although not a portraitist as such, perhaps the most significant artist to visit in Natchez before 1830 was the naturalist John James Audubon. In his *Ornithological Biography*, Audubon has left a vivid description of Natchez as it appeared to him on a "frosty morning" in December. Approaching by flatboat, Audubon could see the same teeming, bustling scene that has been previously described, a scene of the wild, rough-and-tumble life of the flatboat men. While finding that scene "far from being altogether pleasing," the view from the cliffs inspired Audubon to expound on his own particular version of the transcendental vision:

> Vultures unnumbered flew close along the ground on expanded pinions, searching for food; large pines and superb magnolias here and there raised their evergreen tops towards the skies; while on the opposite shores of the Mississippi, vast alluvial beds stretched along, and the view terminated with

the dense forest. Steamers moved rapidly on the broad waters of the great stream; the sunbeams fell with a peculiarly pleasant effect on the distant objects; and as I watched the motions of the White-headed Eagle while pursuing the Fishing Hawk, I thought of the wonderful ways of that Power to whom I too owe my existence."[19]

Audubon thought there was much "romantic scenery" about Natchez, and he relished the dichotomy between the upper and lower cities, breached, in his words, by a "rude causeway." He admired, as well, the prosperity and graciousness of the town, where "wealth and happiness have taken up their abode under most of the planters' roofs, beneath which the wearied traveller or the poor wanderer in search of a resting place, is sure to meet with comfort and relief."[20]

That the artist-naturalist almost assuredly found rest and comfort is demonstrated by two important extant works: a city view attributed to him and a portrait of Benjamin L. C. Wailes. The Wailes family had a plantation across the river on those "vast alluvial beds" Audubon admired, and where he hunted and sketched. Two of his drawings, those of the orchard oriole and the tyrant flycatcher, were later engraved for the volume *Birds of America*.[21] The Wailes portraits (he painted Mr. and Mrs. Levin Wailes and their two sons) are actually chalk drawings in black and grisaille, rather flat and almost caricaturish, as is often the case with Audubon's portraits. The city view, on the other hand, is a smashing composite of rich color combined with a sophisticated grasp of the landscape's contours. Indeed, it is the best view of the city in the entire period.

As I close, I should like to reflect upon the state of Southern studies at this time. If there is a Southern art, then is there a Southern art history? Historians of the caliber of John Demos have established highly-developed methods for the studies of other aspects of American culture. Demos' *A Little Commonwealth* is an excellent study of the objects found in Puritan New England, in their social and philosophic context. But then, in New England one deals with a theocracy of stated intentions and there is a standard, willed by the people, against which their things can be considered.

In the South we are faced with what many non-Southerners call the apologist view. Since the early part of the century, attempts to explain the complexity of Southern history have been seen as efforts to apologize for slavery, or to account for racism. Those are legitimate concerns, but they impact on the art historian in only the vaguest manner. To free the study of southern objects from the didacticism of southern historical polemics, we much acknowledge the manufacture of all goods by a labor class and their consumption by a monied group. A recent worthy effort in that regard is *Plantation Life in Texas* by Elizabeth Silverthorne. In this volume the responsibilities of the labor class are placed into the overall context of plantation function. She makes no attempt to apologize for the unfairness of slavery, but gives considerable attention to the patterns of plantation life and the inter-relations of objects and people.

The issue of race, then, is but one aspect of the larger and more difficult to define nature of southern character. The student of American studies approaches the fabric of national life from a rather detached viewpoint, seeing the events of American life and the objects therein as some kind of phenomenon newly witnessed. In the South we are compelled to think that we have been and remain a people apart. Even when the southern art historian has a sufficient body of information, an accumulation of objects, and well-researched documentation, the questions of southern life will still demand a resolution with the southern character. The "fine old family" dilemma is a lingering scenario. Southerners write about the stuff of the past because they care about that past itself. It is my hope that as we increase the body of knowledge and move farther away from the life of our past the wounds of the South may be healed, and that Southern culture—which, to admit to my chauvinist mood and to echo Genovese, I feel is the deepest and most interesting aspect of the national character—may be seen in the clear light of historical objectivity.

Notes

1. Ulrich B. Phillips, *Life and Labor in the Old South* (Boston: Little Brown, 1963), 217.

2. Eugene D. Genovese, *Roll, Jordan, Roll: The World the Slaves Made* (New York: Random House, 1976), 4.

3. Eugene D. Genovese, "Decline and Fall of a Slaveocrat," *New York Times Book Review*, July 20, 1986, 10.

4. Charles S. Sydnor, *Slavery in Mississippi* (New York: Appleton, 1933), 5.

5. James Weir, "Journal Extract, 1803." Transcript in Natchez History Files, 1800–1819, Mississippi Department of Archives and History.

6. Ben Morgan to David Morgan, September 3, 1800, in *Natchez Democrat*, August 18, 1938.

7. Alexander Wilson to Alexander Lawson, May 18, 1810, in William Edward West Papers, Archives of American Art, Smithsonian Institution.

8. Jonathan Daniels, *The Devil's Backbone: The Story of the Natchez Trace* (New York: McGraw-Hill, 1962), 104–10.

9. Morgan to Morgan, September 3, 1800, in *Natchez Democrat*.

10. Christian Schultz, *Travels on an Inland Voyage through The states of New York, Pennsylvania, Virginia, Ohio, Kentucky, and Tennessee, and through the Territories of Indiana, Louisiana, Mississippi and New Orleans: performed in the years 1807 and 1810* . . . (New York: Isaac Riley, 1810), 132.

11. Weir, "Journal Extract, 1803."

12. John Johnson, "The Natchez Circuit in 1812." Natchez History Files, 1800–19, Mississippi Department of Archives and History.

13. Daniel Smith, "The State of Religion in Natchez in 1816," Natchez History Files, 1800–19, Mississippi Department of Archives and History.

14. *Mississippi Republican*, October 1, 1818.

15. H. Parrott Bacot and Bethany Lambdin, *Natchez-Made Silver of the Nineteenth Century* (Baton Rouge: Anglo-American Museum, 1970).

16. Estill Curtis Pennington, *William Edward West, 1788–1857: Kentucky Painter* (Washington, D.C.: National Portrait Gallery, 1985).

17. William Edward West to Jane West Woods, December 19, 1818, in West Papers, Archives of American Art, Smithsonian Institution.

18. Matthew Harris Jouett to Lawrence Leavey, February 23, 1823, in Archives of American Art, Smithsonian Institution.

19. John James Audubon, *Ornithological Biography or an Account of the Habits of the Birds of America* (Edinburgh: 1831–39), 539.

20. *Ibid.*, 540.

21. *Ibid.*

22. Charles Sackett Sydnor, *Benjamin L. C. Wailes, A Gentleman of the Old Natchez Region* (Durham: Duke University Press, 1938), 129.

Education in Natchez
before 1830

JEANNE MIDDLETON FORSYTHE

Most inquiries into the educational activities of any given time period reveal that the practice of education reflects the society of which it is a part. The schools pass on, from one generation to the next, the values, beliefs, and traditions that have defined that culture. Schooling and education reflect social, political, and economic conditions and in so doing, to a large extent, they also reflect the prejudices and problems of the culture, as well as its achievements and grand legacies. When viewed this way, the study of schools and education becomes an important means of understanding culture: indeed, our inquiry into education in Natchez prior to 1830 provides a singular mirror of many aspects of early Natchez life.

Because an "educational system"—the manner by which a community educates its children and itself—does not spring up overnight, we must consider education in Natchez prior to 1830 from a developmental perspective: the seeds of 1830 Natchez education were sown many, many years earlier. And, because an educational system is not static in its operation, but rather very fluid and dynamic, we must make sure that we chart the changes and tangents that occurred in the development of Natchez education so that we may appreciate the subtleties and peculiarities of its development.

In the broad strokes of Natchez history, the development of education was similar to that in any growing community before 1800—people struggling with limited resources, conflicting interests, and diverse ideas, all trying to meld their common goals. It is, however, only in the fine details of early Natchez, with its immigrant and varied population and its strategic geography, that the unique flavor of that community's educational developments can be seen.

There are few records to document formal educational institutions in the Natchez territory before the early 1800s, but this does not mean that no culture or educational enterprises existed. It suggests that a small population and the demands of simple survival in the wilderness prohibited the successful establishment of formal schooling. But did the practice of education exist? Of course it did.

Consider the Native American community. The tribe from which Natchez takes its name had for generations transferred its knowledge of life in the wilderness to its children. Their values and traditions regarding religion, agriculture, government, and law were cherished through generations and even shared with the first European settlers. As early as 1682, French explorers visited the Natchez region in search of land and opportunities for expansion and wealth. In spite of the initial friendly relations between the Natchez and the Europeans, there came an inevitable clash; by the 1720s, animosity between the two cultures was so intense that war erupted, and by 1731 the Natchez nation had been destroyed.

The Natchez and other tribes in the Natchez territory did not flourish under French or British domination. Neither country regarded the region as a promising producer or consumer market, they did not develop a staple crop, and the Mississippi River did not become a major trading artery during French or British rule. It was not until Spanish rule, beginning in 1779, that the settlers in the Natchez territory began to prosper and subsequently to manifest an interest in more formal education.

Señor Manuel Gayoso de Lemos was named first governor of Spanish Natchez in 1789, and under his leadership more and more settlers came to the Natchez District in search of land and economic privileges not available to them in the eastern United States. Gayoso encouraged the production of tobacco; indigo production boomed, and cotton began to emerge as king. The production of cotton-seed oil was one of Natchez' earliest industries. Cypress logging, livestock, and hemp production were all viable activities as the Natchez economy and community grew.

Although they were under Spanish rule, the people of the Natchez District were not Spanish, but predominantly Anglo-American or African-American. The 1784 census of the Natchez District indicated there were 1,619 people, including 498 black slaves. By 1798 the population had grown to just under 7,000, including 4,500 whites and 2,400 Negroes.[1]

The whites who settled in and around Natchez have been described as aristocratic and intellectual. Although many had been educated in the eastern colleges and in Europe, the primary concerns of economic survival and of taming the rugged environment prohibited any large-scale effort to establish formal schools at home. The usual practice for the wealthy was to employ one or more tutors to come to the home to educate their children; many of Natchez's finer antebellum homes, such as Hope Farm, had a schoolroom included in construction. Often children were sent to New Orleans, to the eastern United States, or to Europe for an education. This provision of education only for those who could afford it surely hampered development of a school system throughout the entire Mississippi Territory, where Natchezeans held powerful political influence.

In April, 1798, the Congress of the United States created the Territory of Mississippi out of the land ceded by Spain. The Natchez District was entering its golden age: The Mississippi River was becoming a vital avenue of traffic in people and commodities, the plantation system was increasing, and the demand for slaves was rising. On a single day in 1790, 260 people arrived by flatboat in Natchez. These 260 people, described as "a typical distribution," included 94 men, 12 women, 37 children, and 117 Negroes. On a typical day, as many as 80 flatboats might be docked in the port, lined up for a mile or more, bearing points of origin from Kentucky, Pennsylvania, Cumberland, South Carolina, Ohio, or Virginia. Natchez was no longer isolated, and as a United States Territory yet to become a state was ruled by frontier politics. History suggests that the printing press was the most viable "educator" of the public at this time. Publishers of the *Mississippi Gazette, Green's Impartial Observer,* and the *Mississippi Herald* demonstrated their interests (though admittedly partisan) in political education.[2]

A good deal is known about the political skirmishes that dominated the affairs of governmental leaders as they participated in the struggle toward statehood, but relatively little is known about the life of an ordinary citizen in Natchez at the beginning of the nineteenth century. Nevertheless, a close look at day-to-day life in Natchez at this time reveals much about the practice of education in the territory. In September, 1800, Ben Morgan wrote to his relatives in Pennsylvania describing the people and the enormous opportunity in Natchez, and noting that the town contains 100 homes and upward, inhabited principally by the storekeepers with a few tradesmen. The country settlement, which extends from 100 to 120 miles along the river and from 20 to 25 miles back, is settled by planters from almost every state in the Union, but principally North and South Carolina and Georgia, cultivating cotton with slaves. . . .

Slaves are in great demand, sell for 400 to 600 dollars. Lands are to be held on credit from 2–10 dollars, according to the distance from water carriage and time of payment. The soil is generally good, but even the thinnest of it, from the moisture and heat of climate, produces abundantly. A man with houseman and two prime slaves in this country would raise off 50 or 60 acres of clear land, cotton enough to sell for 1000 or 1200 dollars, besides raising every article of provision for the support of the family and home. . . .

There are some planters here that have from 1 to 2 hundred head of horses, and from 2–3 hundred head of horned cattle. . . . Tradesmen of every description are in great demand and I can safely say they can earn three times the sum of money in the same length of time here that they can in Pennsylvania.[3]

By 1812 the letters of the Reverend John Johnson of South Carolina, a Methodist minister sent to the Southwest as a missionary, described over one hundred businesses and institutions that developed in the Natchez territory to serve the growing community. These included shops set up by tailors, hatters, boot- and shoemakers, barbers, butchers, bakers, and grocers. Several tradesmen such as brickmasons, plasterers, carpenters, and wagon- and chairmakers established businesses to meet construction needs; and professional men engaged in medicine, teaching, publishing, law, ministry, and banking. At this time, Johnson noted, Natchez had 1500 residents, 450 of whom were slaves.[4]

He also added in his letter that the people were in general, "very rich, very proud, and very polite, exceeding all for compliments, but [had] little humility, little religion, and little piety." As late as 1826 we have Natchez citizens defending the moral character of their town against such reports as those of the Reverend Johnson, and especially against the accusations and comparisons made by "pious Vicksburg." The author of one letter to the editor of a Natchez paper notes five churches in Natchez representing the Roman Catholic, Presbyterian, Methodist, Baptist, and Episcopal denominations.[5]

In the midst of all of this plantation economy, emerging statehood, the entrepeneurial spirit, and under-the-hill life on the river, there was in fact a developing system of schools, a practice of education for nearly every group of Natchez citizens, even those for whom education was legally prohibited. Its development can be traced in the early 1800s through its struggle and growth and change as the political, economic, and social needs of the city and its inhabitants changed.

Mississippi's first constitution stated that "Religion, morality, and knowledge, being necessary to good government, the preservation of liberty, and the happiness of mankind . . . schools and the means of education shall be forever encouraged in this state." The wealthiest and most populated of the state, the Natchez region was most successful in establishing schools. As early as 1803, French clergymen in Natchez advertised in *The Constitution Conservator* the establishment of a French school "for all these who are desirous of learning the French language." The records of St. Paul's Episcopal Church, established in Woodville, Mississippi, in 1823 by the Reverend James Angel Fox, indicate that he taught school as well as conducted services twice a month. The parish register notes that "Mr. Fox from the beginning of his ministry depended for the chief part of the support of his family upon teaching a school."[6]

Throughout the early 1800s *The Mississippi Republican and Literary Register* and *The Mississippi State Gazette* regularly carried advertisements of schools and tutors available to male and female children of the city. The ads typically described the curriculum, tuition, location, and lodging facilities, if available. Whereas these schools charged tuition, often requiring payment in advance, less fortunate children could join the regular enrollment of the Natchez Orphan Asylum, which instructed them in basic reading, spelling, and writing.[7]

There were three types of schooling in Natchez before 1830 that represent different approaches to education and which help to define the culture at this time. The first—that promoted by the Elizabeth Female Academy—is interesting for its uniqueness in purpose, its twenty-six-year success, and its still-controversial claim to being the first of its kind. The second—that of Jefferson College—reflects through its life, beginning in 1802, the changing interests and attitudes of the middle and planter classes in Mississippi from the early and flush times to the Civil War and after. The third type of schooling—the education of the Negro, both slave and free—did not take place in an established institution but was clearly a significant practice.

One of the myths of Southern history, and one particularly associated with the Natchez region, is that all white women aspired to be the stereotypical plantation mistress and therefore spent all of their time mastering needlepoint, the mint julep, and the twenty-two-inch waistline. And although some of the ladies who attended Elizabeth Female

Academy surely possessed these skills and attribues, its establishment and success demonstrate that many young women were afforded the benefits of a liberal education during a very early time when this was not a common practice.

Elizabeth Female Academy was established in 1819 on 104 acres of land deeded by Elizabeth Roach and her husband. Through its twenty-six-year history, the academy's annual enrollment varied from approximately twenty-five to sixty students. Tuition varied depending on the inclusion of board. Although the Mississippi Conference of the Methodist Church filled many of the seats on the governing board, the academy was not a school for religious training in Methodism. Instead, according to one supporter, "Only the general principles of the Christian religion, with an application of them to practice" were emphasized. The course of study included English grammar, arithmetic, geography, astronomy, chemistry, and Latin or French if desired. The young ladies could also receive training in voice or instrumental music. Students who completed a full course of study would be entitled to the degree *Domina Scientiarom*.[8]

There is controversy over whether Elizabeth Female Academy was the first institution of higher education in the United States to confer a degree upon a female. Some scholars, arguing that the academy was not a college but a secondary preparatory school, claim that this honor goes to Wesleyan College in Georgia; others maintain that the academy's program of study was in fact at the collegiate level. To this controversy must also be added the fact that many of the records surrounding the history of the academy have been destroyed, and the remainder are so fragmentary that it is difficult to tell whether an undergraduate degree was ever conferred.[9] Elizabeth Female Academy is known to have provided a valuable and unusual service to young women interested in a liberal education on the frontier.

Jefferson College, founded in 1802 by an act of the legislature of the Mississippi Territory, at the urging of a few "men of prominence" and "men of learning," stands as a testimony to the resiliency of the human spirit. Because the founders believed that "Education conduces to the happiness and improvement of man and is particularly necessary to the support and purity of Republican Government," the college was established to stand, in Governor W. C. C. Claiborne's terms, "as a bulwark against luxury and vice." Claiborne hoped that "the community of youths at the seminary . . . would form those ties of friendship and brotherhood so essential to the infant American republic."[10] After some struggle over a location (with Greenville being the chief competitor), the town of Washington, seven miles west of Natchez, was selected.

The school had difficulty getting started. Money was hard to come by, and good teachers, who generally had problems collecting their salaries from the parents, were hard to keep. The school day began at 6:00 A.M.; there was an hour recess for breakfast at 8:00; students attended class from 9:00 to 1:00, had a 2-hour lunch break, then continued in class until the sun was "half-an-hour-high." On Sunday, students were expected to dress and to go to church. School vacations were in August and for 2 weeks at Christmas. Tuition in 1820 was $32 for the long session plus an additional $140 for board; by 1830 tuition had risen to $60 for the long session, though the board charge remained at $140. In 1818 almost one-third of the 66 students were female, but by 1820 females no longer attended Jefferson, going instead to Elizabeth Female Academy. By 1839 Jefferson's enrollment stood at 81.

Initially, the curriculum included the study of Cicero, Virgil, Homer, Greek oration, rhetoric, New Testament, arithmetic, algebra, history, geography, logic, geometry, and science. During the senior year, students reviewed the ancient writers, and focused primarily on scientific study, including geography, astronomy, and chemistry, moral and political philosophy, natural philosophy, and the philosophy of the human mind.

Through the years, the course of study took on a more practical and scientific emphasis, and classes in subjects considered more useful to this particular frontier society, such as French and Spanish, advanced math, and engineering, were included. By 1840 a student could pursue two basic courses of study: the Full Course included the traditional classical education and scientific studies, whereas the Partial Course, called the English and Scientific Course, included little of the classics.

Most of the young men who attended Jefferson College in the 1820s and 1830s were of local origin, from Adams and Washington counties. Many were from quite wealthy families. During the early 1830s the college began to reflect a growing military emphasis under the direction of President E. B. Williston and Major John Holbrook. Students were required to wear cadet uniforms and were trained in the use of muskets, artillery, and swords.

As the school gained strength and reputation, it also played a larger role in the life of the Natchez community. The most impressive educational institution in the Natchez region, Jefferson College was the center of intellectual pursuits. Trustees William Dunbar, Benjamin Wailes, and

John Monette formed the Mississippi Society for the Acquirement and Dissemination of Useful Knowledge. The Washington Polemic Association and the Adams Athenaeum both requested the use of Jefferson College rooms for library and reading rooms. By 1837 the Jefferson College and Washington Lyceum was created in the hope that "an association of gentlemen of different pursuits and professions and acquirements into a society, would be an efficient means of collecting much valuable information on subjects which neither time nor facilities permitted each fully to investigate."[11] The Lyceum's committees covered *belles-lettres*, mental science, moral philosophy, theology, constitutional law, political economy, natural history, math, physical science, history, and anatomy and physiology. The Lyceum held regular meetings which, though open to the public, were usually attended only by board members.

Although the next distinct period in the history of Jefferson College falls beyond 1830, it is worth briefly noting a change in society that was reflected in the college's curriculum. Following the depression in 1837 Natchez intellectuals were forced to turn their attention to practical matters and subsequently organized the Agricultural, Botanical, and Horticultural Society of Jefferson College in 1839. With an interest in agricultural improvement, they gave little attention to the development of a staple crop, and instead placed great emphasis on vegetables and fruits, farm machinery, farming techniques, cotton baling, local manufacturing, and home building. Soon the interest in agriculture grew to include livestock—horses, cows, sheep, and hogs.

Jefferson College continued to serve the Natchez region and the state until the Civil War. It was occupied by Union troops for a short while, then returned to the trustees in 1865. Although the college did not enjoy the same degree of success in the years following the Civil War that it had in the early 1800s, it was a very valuable institution in the early Natchez territory and has left a legacy for all of Mississippi.

The third significant aspect of education in Natchez before 1830 is the education of the black population in the Natchez territory, both slave and free. In Adams county in 1800 there were 2,248 whites and 2,412 blacks, of whom 155 were free. By 1840 there were 4,910 whites and 14,524 blacks, including 283 free.[12] Just as many have labored under the myths associated with the lifestyles and aspirations of the Southern white woman, so too have many of us labored to dispel the myths associated with the intelligence and character of the black man and woman at this time. It is true that at this time in history any formal

131

education was prohibited blacks in Mississippi as in other southern states. How then do we account for those blacks who were educated men and women of character? What kind of education was afforded the black, slave and free, prior to 1830?

The slave laws of Mississippi stated that "all meetings or assemblies of slaves or of free negroes or mulattoes, mixing and associating with such slaves, above the number of five, at any place of public resort, or at any meeting house or house in the night, or at any school or schools, for teaching them reading or writing, either in the day or night, under whatsoever pretext" would be unlawful.[13]

There were numerous violations of rules prohibiting the education of slaves. First of all, it was quite common for the slaveholder to teach an individual slave to read and write. House servants, as well as those servants who worked in the fields or in town, were often trained in ways the slave system prohibited—as artisans, builders, carpenters, black-smiths, weavers, seamstresses, quartermasters, machinists, account-ants, and in other areas that required trained hands, skilled minds, discipline, and character. Mississippians are familiar with the story of Isaiah T. Montgomery who, while a slave of Jefferson Davis' brother Joseph, was instructed in the basic skills and trained to be the con-fidential accountant of the plantation. Charles Sydnor describes an advertisement for a school for Negro children which appeared in a Washington, Mississippi, paper in which Mr. T. Washington Jones of-fered to teach reading, writing, and arithmetic to Negro children and adults, though it is not clear whether he intended to teach slave or free blacks. At any rate, Jones was apparently informed that his intentions were unacceptable; his public advertisement may have been the most objectionable fact about Jones' plans to instruct blacks. Nat Turner's rebellion made it absolutely clear that "knowledge and slavery were incompatible."[14]

Another indication that some slaves received an education in spite of written prohibitions against it can be found in those legal documents which record the conditions surrounding the manumission of a slave. When young William Johnson, a free man of color known as the Barber of Natchez, was granted his freedom at age eleven in 1820 by his owner William Johnson, Section 2 of the act of the Mississippi legislature stated that "the said William Johnson shall educate, or cause to be educated, and maintain, or cause to be maintained, said child until he arrives at the age of 21 years."[15] Clearly there was at least some sentiment that allowed and even encouraged persons of color to be educated. It is this paradox of the slave system that Henry Bullock suggests provided a hidden passage through which slaves gained access to education and leadership.

A third indication that some slaves had access to the rudiments of an education can be found by examining the character and training of the slave population itself. Several records show that many blacks who were sold into slavery were well educated men and women, of substantial means and background. A special example is the West African prince sold into slavery to the Thomas family of Natchez. His character, disposition, and outlook on life influenced all who knew him, both slave and free, black and white.[16] We cannot begin to measure how he, and other slaves of similar background and character, influenced and educated those slaves in his company.

The Natchez territory had one of the highest concentrations of free people of color in the country. Blacks who were educated, often quite wealthy, and usually well informed regarding the events of the day, moved with relative freedom in the Natchez territory before 1830. William Johnson, and others like him, could educate and be educated, though always remembering to be discreet. After 1830, following the Nat Turner rebellion and other slave insurrections across the South, slave owners voiced much more concern about the adverse consequences of educating slaves, and prohibitions against educating slaves became much more severe. Bullock suggests, however, that the hidden passage had already been opened, the seeds of the black educated class had already been sown. The relationships that developed between slave and slave owner, between whites and persons of color, in what was designed to be an ascetic, cost-effective, and profit-driven economic system grew into something much more than any of the actors in the scenario could have imagined. These relationships, says Bullock, "carried a degree of personal intimacy that reached beyond the level of blood mixture and miscegenation into the area of cultural diffusion and acculturation. They constituted a way of life that transformed many Negro children into personality types quite unlike those prescribed by the rational order."[17]

Natchez before 1830 was as diverse as the tributaries of the Mississippi that converged at its door, a region so rich and colorful that visitors continue to travel from around the world to experience its unique character, a town so peculiar that to capsulize its educational legacy remains a difficult task. Natchezans still treasure Elizabeth Female Academy, Jefferson College, William Johnson and the spirit and love of knowledge each of these three represents. Perhaps the real treasure of

Natchez lies in how the twentieth-century city interprets its history and educates its youth regarding what Natchez represented in its first golden years and how that legacy continues to shape us today.

Notes

1. Jack D. L. Holmes, *Gayoso: The Life of a Spanish Governor in the Mississippi Valley, 1789–1799* (Baton Rouge: Louisiana State University Press, 1965), 114–17.

2. D. Clayton James, *Antebellum Natchez* (Baton Rouge: Louisiana State University Press, 1968), 41; R. A. McLemore (ed.), *A History of Mississippi* (Hattiesburg: University and College Press of Mississippi, 1973).

3. "Natchez History, 1800–1819," letter on file, Mississippi Department of Archives and History.

4. *Ibid.*

5. *Ibid.*, "Natchez History 1820-1860," *ibid.*

6. *Mississippi, Constitution, 1817*, Art. VI, Sec. 16; [Natchez] *Constitution Conservator*, Saturday April 16, 1803, 1, No. 27, p. 4. Mississippi Department of Archives and History Microfilm, Misc. roll #5; *St. Paul's Episcopal Church, Woodville, Mississippi, October 4, 1823–October 4, 1923*, Mississippi Department of Archives and History. The Reverend Fox also served as president of Jefferson College at Washington, Mississippi, in 1848. See "The Episcopal Church in Mississippi from the Beginning to 1976," *Sesquicentennial Council: The Episcopal Diocese of Mississippi, 1826–1976*, Trinity Episcopal Church, Natchez, MS, January 30–31, February 1, 1976. The first Catholic school in Mississippi, the Academy for Young Ladies, was opened in Natchez under the auspices of Bishop Chanche in 1841. See Di Michele and Charles Conrad, "The History of the Roman Catholic Educational System in Mississippi." (dissertation, Mississippi State University, 1973).

7. Natchez Orphan Asylum, *Annual Report*, 1826, in "Natchez History 1820–1860," Mississippi Department of Archives and History.

8. Subject File (Jumbo) "Elizabeth Female Academy," Mississippi Department of Archives and History.

9. *Ibid.*

10. W. M. Drake, *An Outline of the History of Jefferson Military College, Chronology and Comment* (Washington, Miss.: n.p., n.d.), 7; W. T. Blain, *Education in the Old Southwest: A History of Jefferson College* (Washington, Miss.; n.p., n.d.), 1.

11. *Ibid.*, 103.

12. *Census Report*, Adams County, Miss., 1800–60.

13. *Goodspeed's Biographical and Historical Memoirs of Mississippi* (2 vols.; Chicago: Goodspeed, 1891), 96.

14. See Henry A. Bullock, *The Education of the Negro in the South from 1619 to the Present* (New York: Praeger, 1967). J. Loewen, C. Sallis, J. Middleton [Forsythe] (eds.) *Mississippi: Conflict and Change* (New York: Pantheon, 1974), 187. Charles S. Sydnor,

Slavery in Mississippi (Baton Rouge: Louisiana State University Press, 1959), 54; Letter to the editor, signed "citizen." *Woodville Republican,* December 22, 1832.

15. *Laws of the State of Mississippi,* passed by the General Assembly, 3rd Sess. (Natchez, 1820), 38. See also *Mississippi State Gazette,* February 12, 1820.

16. See Terry Alford, *Prince Among Slaves* (New York: Harcourt-Brace Jovanovich, 1977).

17. Bullock, *Education of the Negro in the South,* p. 8.

The Architecture of Natchez before 1830

Samuel Wilson, Jr.

Natchez derived its name from the Indian tribe that the French explorer Pierre Le Moyne d'Iberville first visited in 1700; he noted that "of all the savages, they are the most civilized nation." Iberville's brother, Jean-Baptiste Le Moyne de Bienville, returned in 1715 and had a fort built there which he named Rosalie in honor of the Comtesse de Pontchartrain. This was the beginning of the architectural development of Natchez. Two major French concessions were soon established, one called St. Catherine and the other La Terre Blanche, or the White Earth. Smaller plantations were also built by various individuals, including the historian Le Page du Pratz. These first settlers built simple buildings of timber frames enclosed with wide boards and generally roofed with shingles. All of these, however, were destroyed when the Natchez Indians revolted and massacred the French in November, 1729. Only the fort was rebuilt, and French settlers never returned to the area.

Following the defeat of the French by the British in the French and Indian wars, all of the French colony east of the Mississippi (except New Orleans), including the Natchez area, was surrendered to England in 1763. Natchez became part of the new British province of West Florida, which had its capital at Pensacola. Large land grants were made to English settlers coming from the Eastern seaboard. Fort Rosalie was rebuilt and renamed Fort Panmure, and the new settlers began to build simple frame houses, generally gable-ended and with galleries, not unlike Mount Locust, built some years later on the Natchez Trace (fig. 1). A provision of some of these early British land grants required the

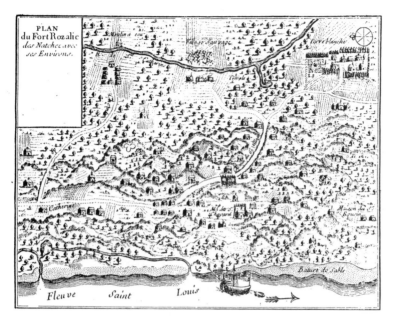

Fig. 1. Plan of Fort Rosalie and the early French settlements at Natchez. From Dumont de Montigny's *Memoire Historique*.

recipient to erect "one good dwelling house to contain at least twenty feet in length and sixteen in breadth," the same dimensions as the main frame of Mount Locust. No town was laid out by the British, either on the bluff or "under the hill."

Anthony Hutchins, a settler from South Carolina, received a grant to the White Apple Village tract in 1772, and his son John later wrote that at the time "Natchez was a wilderness, a canebrake. . . . Our houses were very rude and rough, built and covered without nail or hammer . . . it was the constant practice of neighbors to assist each other in . . . putting up houses."[1] None of these houses "in the English manner" is known still to exist.

During the American Revolution, Spain, which had received from France the Louisiana province west of the Mississippi and New Orleans, supported the American cause. The Spanish governor, Don Bernardo de Gálvez, captured the British forts at Manchac and Baton Rouge, and Natchez was surrendered to Spain in 1779. Later, Gálvez also drove the British from Mobile and Pensacola. Spanish authority was established in Natchez and lasted until 1798, but few Spaniards settled in the area; the cultural pattern remained essentially British, and houses continued to be built in the same "English manner."

137

The principal Spanish contribution to the architectural history of Natchez was the laying out of the town on the bluff around 1790. The plan was probably done by Carlos Trudeau, official Spanish surveyor, and laid out on the site by William Dunbar, assistant surveyor of the district.[2] Before that, in the 1780s a few streets had been laid out under the hill, probably by the Spanish commandant, Francisco Collel. It was in this lower town that the first Natchez houses were built. Among these were "a frame dwelling house" that Richard Harrison sold to Thomas Green on September 14, 1782, for $600, and "two dwelling houses, two storehouses and a kitchen, including a billiard table" that "Don Miguel Eslava, a store keeper of this Fort," bought for $800 from Richard Bacon on March 6, 1783.

In January, 1788, three Irish priests newly arrived in New Orleans were sent to Natchez and the Spanish governor, Esteban Miro, requested that Natchez commandant, Don Carlos de Grand Pré, select a suitable site for a church. The site selected was a 300-acre tract bought by Esteban Minor from Richard Harrison, to whom it had been granted in 1782.[3] In a letter to Grand Pré of January 7, 1788, Miro wrote regarding the site: "There is one in the immediate vicinity of the fort which belongs to Don Esteban Minor, its Intendant, upon which are constructed various buildings, and among them a house of fifty feet of length by forty of width with galleries, divided into a large hall and five rooms with separate kitchen, stable and storehouse, situated on three hundred square arpents of land on which a city could be laid out. All could be bought for two thousand hard silver pesos."[4]

The site was purchased by the Spanish government on April 5, 1788, and Minor's buildings became the residence of the Irish priests. That streets were laid out around these buildings may be the reason that the blocks between Main and State streets are much larger than the others. When the Natchez area became part of the United States in 1798, the Catholic priests left for other areas still under Spanish rule, and their former residence was claimed by the United States as having belonged to the former sovereign, Carlos IV of Spain. This priest's house was later given by Congress to the city of Natchez, together with the promenade or park on the bluff. The house then became the courthouse and served until a new brick building was erected on the site in 1817.

The church was built at some distance from the priest's house, a site on Commerce Street, between Main and Franklin. The building was designed by Gilberto Guillemard, the architect who designed the

Cabildo, Cathedral, and Presbytère in New Orleans, based on the design of the first New Orleans church designed by Adrien de Pauger in 1724 and destroyed in the great fire of March 21, 1788. The contract for this first Natchez church was signed before the notary Rafael Perdomo in New Orleans on March 30, 1790.[5] The contractor was François Langlois who, on the same day, signed a contract to build a hospital on the Natchez bluff. It was intended that the square in front of the church—the square now bounded by Commerce, Main, Pearl, and Franklin—be left open as a public square, and it was left unnumbered on the early plans of the town. Unfortunately, it was soon sold off in lots and built upon.

In a letter dated January 6, 1792, Don Manuel Gayoso de Lemos, Spanish governor of Natchez, wrote to the provincial governor at New Orleans that "last year [1791] we drew up plans for a city adjacent to the fort of Natchez. There were some houses already constructed on this site. Since then a church and a hospital have been constructed. In the course of the present year [1792] we intend to increase the number of houses to thirty."[6]

Besides the buildings of Esteban Minor that became the priest's house and later the courthouse, there were probably also the buildings erected by Major James Wiley, a Revolutionary War veteran who arrived in Natchez in 1788. His son, George Wiley, who came as a one-year-old child with his father, later wrote that "at that time there were but two or three houses on the hill. . . . The houses built by the first settlers on the hill were mere shanties. . . . Probably the oldest house now [ca. 1871] existing in Natchez is the one now occupied by Mrs. Postlethwaite, on Jefferson street, between Union and Rankin. It was at one time kept as a tavern by a man named King."[7]

Wiley's father also had conducted a tavern in his house soon after his arrival in 1788. It was located at what is now 609 Franklin Street, also between Union and Rankin, and it is probable that the buildings of Wiley's Tavern were moved after 1807 a block away to Jefferson Street and reconstructed to become King's Tavern (fig. 2). According to the tax list of 1807, the site on Jefferson Street where King's Tavern now stands was then vacant. George Wiley wrote that "my father's house was on the lot now occupied by the store of Wm. Earhart [now 609 Franklin], and all north of that was in woods." If King's Tavern is actually Wiley's Tavern, relocated, it would indeed be the oldest house in Natchez, possibly built even before the streets of the town were laid out in 1791.

Besides the hospital, a governor's house was erected on the bluff, according to William Dunbar, who noted that "Governor Gayoso caused a large building to be erected for his own residence, at his private expense, but before it was finished it was blown down by a hurricane."[8]

Gayoso then built Concord on a site that he bought in 1794 which was, according to Daniel Clark, "a most valuable tract . . . on which he built and called the place Concord which he now [1798] values at $20,000."[9] Concord, when first built in the Spanish colonial period, probably looked somewhat like the house on Ellicott Hill, long known as Connelly's Tavern (fig. 3). The columned galleries and curving granite stairways were probably added by the architect Levi Weeks after Concord was acquired by Esteban Minor after Gayoso's death in 1799.[10] This great house was destroyed by fire in 1901 (fig. 4).

William Dunbar's plantation house, The Forest, below Natchez was one of the important houses of the Spanish period, but no drawings of the original house are known to exist. The house was rebuilt in 1817; the new house with a surrounding colonnade, probably designed by Levi Weeks, was destroyed by fire in 1852.

William Dunbar also designed a two-story jail to be built in Natchez in 1798. His drawing, in the Spanish archives in Simancas, Spain, shows a two-story rectangular frame building with gable ends surrounded by galleries with slender wood columns, over which the roof extends at a lower pitch, a roof form similar to that of Connelly's Tavern.[11]

That house on Ellicott Hill (fig. 5), headquarters of the Natchez Garden Club, was built as his residence by James Moore, who purchased the site in 1797.[12] A gallery with slender turned wood columns on both upper and lower stories extends across the front and may have originally continued around the sides and rear, later enclosed to form rather narrow rooms with lower ceilings than the central room of the house. The steep gable-end roof framed over this large central room is extended at a lesser pitch over the narrow rooms across the ends and rear of the house. This distinctive double-pitch roof is characteristic of late eighteenth- and early nineteenth-century Natchez houses.

The fine scale and delicate details of the interior woodwork in cornices, door casings, and mantels, with elaborate reeding and gouge work, recall details of late eighteenth-century east coast houses; they set a standard of excellence for Natchez millwork until the 1830s. In the late eighteenth century, brick was available in Nachez and was used principally for foundation and basement walls and for the large chimneys often found on both ends of frame houses, as at Connelly's Tavern.

Another notable example of the architecture of the late Spanish

Fig. 2. King's Tavern on Jefferson
Street
Frank W. Masson

Fig. 3. Concord, the mansion built for Don Manuel Gayoso de Lemos

Fig. 4. Exterior stairways of Concord after the house burned in 1901
Richard Koch

Fig. 5. The House on Ellicott Hill (Connelly's Tavern)
Richard Koch

colonial period is Hope Farm, once the residence of Don Carlos de Grand Pré, Spanish governor of Natchez between 1781 and 1794. The main part of the house, with a low-pitched roof extending over front and rear galleries, has been extensively remodeled in the Greek Revival style of the 1840s and 1850s. The basic exterior form of the house, however, retains its original colonial character.

None of the Natchez houses of the Spanish colonial era contains any of the elements popularly associated with the architecture of that period such as wrought-iron grilles and balconies, tile roofs, and round arches. Instead the buildings are basically Anglo-American in character, with some French influences from neighboring Louisiana.

The Territorial Period—1798–1817

As the result of negotiations between Spain and the United States, the boundary between the two territories was set at the 31st parallel (the present boundary between Mississippi and Louisiana) and on March 30, 1798, the Spanish garrison withdrew from Fort Panmure, and Natchez became American, in the Mississippi Territory as created by an act of Congress of April 7, 1798. The American population rapidly increased, and in the years following as wealth, principally from cotton, also increased, new and more substantial houses, many of brick, were built. In 1808 Silas Brown wrote that "Natchez is a very brisk place for business and appears to be rapidly increasing both as to trade and improvements in building. But at present the buildings are, generally speaking, low and mean. There is not a house in the whole place that may be said to be elegant."[13] Of the 133 buildings on the 1805 tax rolls, only Mañuel Texada's house at the corner of Wall and Washington streets was noted as being built of brick, and it was valued at $12,000.

Texada had purchased the site for his house in 1798 and probably began construction soon after. The house was leased as a hotel and city tavern to William H. Beaumont, who advertised in December, 1805, that he had moved "into Mr. Manuel Texada's large, elegant and commodious new brick house. The house is superior when finished, to any other in the territory."[14] The plan of this two-story house was unusual, with a large center room extending from front to back, with two nearly square rooms on each side and a gallery across the rear. The center room was described as "an elegant Hall or Dancing Room which is now used for the Dancing assemblies."

The house, which became the American Eagle Tavern in 1806, has been restored by its present owners, Dr. and Mrs. George Moss. The

143

handsome entrance doorway with its semicircular fan transom was salvaged from another early brick house, Burling Hill, which was demolished (its site is now occupied by the Presbyterian Sunday School on State and Pearl streets).

Burling Hill, built about the same time as Texada, was listed as unfinished on the 1805 tax roll. These two early brick houses were somewhat similar in form, with hipped roofs and well-detailed wood cornices. Both had five openings across the front, with a central entrance doorway. Their wood details, like those of Connelly's Tavern, are well designed, fine in scale, with gouge work, reeding, dentils, and other moldings and carvings in their ornamentation.

Among other early nineteenth-century houses finished with this same delicacy of detail is the one called the Priest's House (fig. 6), because it was built on part of the half of Square No. 10 that was granted to Father Francis Lennan in 1794 as a garden, and sold by him when he left Natchez with the Spanish garrison in 1798. This small two-story gable-end frame house was apparently built between 1805 and 1809 by James Andrews, who bought the 25-foot-wide lot that extended from Main Street back to the courthouse lots before Market Street was cut through the square. Andrews paid $2,400 in 1805 for this long, narrow lot with a house at its Main Street end, and in 1809 he sold the rear half of the lot to David B. Morgan for $8,000—an indication that a new house had been built on it.[15] After Andrews died in 1811, his estate paid to Alexander Miller, a builder, an amount still owed "in full balance for building new house under contract with deceased."[16]

During these early years of the territorial period, houses of similar quality and character were being built in the country around Natchez, especially in the new town of Washington, a few miles west, that became the territorial capital. Among those still standing is Fletcher's Tavern, built about 1801, now in ruinous condition but with traces of its territorial architectural character in its reeded mantels and other details. It was apparently built by Ebenezer Reese who acquired the site for $80 in 1801 and sold it in 1808 to Charles Defrance for $6,000.[17] It was thought that this was the house in which the territorial legislature met in 1815, for a document signed by Defrance states that "I . . . have rented my house . . . for the use of the Territorial Legislature to commence on the 27th of December 1814." At that date, however, Defrance no longer owned this house, which was bought in April, 1814, by Charles Miles who leased and then sold it to Richard Fletcher as a tavern house in February, 1815.[18]

144

Fig. 6. The "Priest's House," removed from 311 Market Street
Richard Koch

Fig. 7. The Rapalje-Mercer House at Wall and State streets, under restoration
Frank W. Masson

Another excellent example of an early nineteenth-century house in Washington is Meadvilla, built about 1808 by Cowles Mead, secretary and acting territorial governor of Mississippi. Its design and delicate interior details of mantels, cornices, chair rails, and door and window casings are of exceptional quality. In 1813 the house was advertised as "a House of Entertainment, known as the Washington Hotel, at the sign of the Spread Eagle . . . in the large and commodious house formerly occupied by Colonel Cowles Mead."[19] A west wing was added to the house in the 1850s, and other alterations and additions have been made since. Washington, in 1808, was described by an Englishman, Fortescue Cummings, as a town "in which I counted thirty scattering houses, including one store, one apothecary's shop, three taverns and a gaol."[20] Taverns were an important commodity to the traveler of that day.

Perhaps the most important event in the architectural development of Natchez was the arrival before 1809 of Levi Weeks, a native of Massachusetts who soon became the most noted architect in Natchez. Weeks probably completed houses already under construction, such as Burling Hill where he signed his name on the back of a panel of the entrance door jamb, the doorway that was placed on Texada Tavern after Burling Hill was demolished. He may also have been responsible for the addition

146

of the columns and porticos on older houses such as Gloster and Concord. In 1815 Weeks built the brick First Presbyterian Church and in 1817 designed the east wing, the first permanent building for Jefferson College.[21] The contractor for the church and the college buildings was Lewis Evans. Weeks may also have designed the house at State and Wall streets that was built about 1819 for Mrs. Jane Ellis Rapalje and inherited by her niece, Mrs. William Newton Mercer, in 1820 (fig. 7). The house, now in the process of restoration, is unusual in Natchez and similar to Savannah houses of the period.[22]

The most significant work of Levi Weeks was the building of Auburn (fig. 8) for Lyman Harding in 1812. Additions to each side of Auburn and the rear colonnade were made after the house was acquired by Stephen Duncan in 1827. In a letter dated September 27, 1812, to a friend in Massachusetts, Weeks wrote about his building activities and the construction of Auburn:

> My employment is the superintendence of a large brick house and a brick Presbyterian Church as architect. . . . I have also been employed the season past to give plans for an hospital and banking house. . . . I last year built an excellent two story brick house, 2nd rate fireproof. . . . The brick house I am now building is just without the city line and is designed for the most magnificent building in the Territory. The body of this house is 60 by 45 feet with a portico of 31 feet projecting 12 feet supported by 4 Ionic columns with the Corinthian entablature, the ceiling vaulted, the house two stories with a geometrical staircase to ascend to the second story. This is the first house in the Territory on which was ever attempted any of the orders of Architecture. The site is one of those peculiar situations which combines all the delight of romance, the pleasures of rurality, and the approach of sublimity. I am the more particular in describing this seat not only to give you an idea of the progress of improvement but to inform you what you will hear with pleasure that the owner of it is a Yankey, a native of our own state, Massachusetts and is now in Boston on a visit. His name Lyman Harding.[23]

Weeks added that "the town has been supplied by the water from the Mississippi, until of late. There are 3 wells and a great number of cisterns, introduced by your humble servant." These are the underground domed brick cisterns, a number of which still remain in Natchez.

Levi Weeks was certainly the most important and influential architect of the territorial period, which ended with the admission of Mississippi as a state in 1817. In that same year Weeks may have been the architect for The Forest, built for the widow of William Dunbar on the site of his earlier house a few miles south of Natchez. This house was of particular

Fig. 8. Auburn, designed by Levi Weeks, architect, 1812
Richard Koch

significance, for it was the first known example in the area of a house with a surrounding two-story colonnade. Unfortunately, The Forest burned in 1852, and only a few of its columns remain to mark the site.[24] When Weeks died in 1819 the inventory of his estate listed at least eleven books on architecture, including William Salmon's *Palladio Londinensis;* design elements from these books were incorporated in his buildings.[25]

Another of the major Natchez mansions that may have been designed by Levi Weeks is Monmouth, built about 1818 for John Hankinson.[26] Like Levi Weeks's east wing of Jefferson College, Monmouth was originally of red brick with marble keystones over the windows, and the circular head entrance doorway is flanked by two narrow windows instead of sidelights. This same unusual treatment is also found at Gloster and may be the result of alterations and additions made to the house of Winthrop Sargent, first territorial governor of Mississippi. The front of Monmouth was radically changed by the addition of a heavy Greek Revival portico by its later owner General John A. Quitman, but most of the fine-scaled details of the early nineteenth century remain on the interior.

In 1822 the artist-naturalist John James Audubon painted a great panorama of Natchez as it then appeared.[27] To the left of center appears Clifton, the only one of the great Natchez mansions that was destroyed during the Civil War.[28] On his arrival in Natchez, Audubon noted in his journal that "the Theatre, a poor framed building and a new and elegant mansion [Clifton] the property of Mr. Postlethwaite attract the anxious eye." To its right in the painting is the large brick building, a hotel known as Travellers Hall, finished in 1820 and destroyed by the tornado of 1840. Near it is the steep-roofed, red brick Texada Tavern and the red-brick domed courthouse completed in 1821, replacing the old house of the Spanish clergy that had been used as the courthouse since 1798.

Among the several churches shown in Audubon's panorama, the domed red-brick Trinity Episcopal Church appears at the far right of the picture. In the 1840s it was remodeled in the Greek Revival style, the dome and cupola being removed and a fine Doric pedimented portico added. On the interior some details of the 1820s, including the delicately molded and paneled circular head window casings, have been maintained.

Shortly after Audubon's painting was completed, Peter Little's mansion, Rosalie (fig. 9), at the end of the esplanade opposite Clifton, was built with bricks from the kilns that appear in the foreground of the

Fig. 9. Rosalie, home of the Daughters of the American Revolution
Tebbs & Knell, 1925

picture. This important document of the appearance of Natchez before 1830 hung for many years at Melrose, but unfortunately was removed from Mississippi some years ago by heirs of the late owner, Mrs. George M. Kelly.

Andrew Brown, an architect from Scotland, arrived in Natchez around 1820 and soon became associated with Peter Little, the owner of Rosalie. In 1828 he purchased Little's sawmill and operated it successfully for many years. Brown was the architect in 1827 for a handsome Masonic Temple (fig. 10) that formerly stood diagonally opposite St. Mary's Cathedral at Main and Union streets and was demolished in 1890.[29] He also designed his own residence, Magnolia Vale, and laid out its elaborate gardens, notable for years as Brown's Gardens. The house burned in the 1940s, and a new house designed by Richard Koch, incorporating some ideas from the earlier house, was erected on its foundations for Howard Peabody, a direct descendant of Andrew Brown.

Although the design of Peter Little's Rosalie is generally attributed to his brother-in-law, James S. Griffin of Baltimore, this attribution is undocumented. It is possible that Little's associate, Andrew Brown, may have had a part in its design. Brown may also have been the architect for

Fig. 10. Old Masonic Temple, designed by Andrew Brown, architect, 1827; demolished 1890

the First Presbyterian Church, built about 1829 to replace the earlier Levi Weeks brick church of 1815.

Numerous other important Natchez houses were built in the prosperous decades between 1810 and 1830. These were all characterized by well-designed and fine-scaled details of both interior and exterior millwork. Many of these houses had handsome entrance doorways with elliptical fan transoms and sidelights. These include The Briars, apparently built between 1814 and 1818 for Arthur Mahan; Holly Hedges, built or extensively remodeled about 1818 for Edward Turner; Hawthorne; Linden; the Griffith-McComas House; the Presbyterian Manse; Cottage Gardens; Fair Oaks; and others of this period besides Rosalie and the Mercer House already mentioned. So popular in Natchez was this form of entrance doorway that even after the Greek Revival style replaced the earlier federal forms, when D'Evereux, one of the purest Greek Revival examples, was built about 1840, the rear entrance doorway was designed in the pre-1830s style.

Although few eighteenth-century buildings remain in Natchez, those built in the early nineteenth century, in the years before 1830, established a standard of architectural excellence that continued through the century and into present times.

Notes

1. John Q. Anderson (ed.), "The Narrative of John Hutchins," *Journal of Mississippi History* (January, 1958), 3.

2. Mrs. Dunbar Rowland, *Life, Letters and Papers of William Dunbar* (Jackson: Mississippi Historical Society, 1930), 76.

3. Acts of Rafael Perdomo, April 5, 1788, New Orleans Notarial Archives (hereinafter cited as NONA).

4. Mississippi Provincial Archives, Spanish Domination (hereinafter cited as MPA-SD), III, 217, in Mississippi Department of Archives and History, Jackson.

5. Acts of Rafael Perdomo, March 30, 1790, NONA.

6. MPA-SD, IV, 6.

7. George Wiley, "Natchez in the Olden Times," in J. F. H. Claiborne, *Mississippi as a Province, Territory and State* (Jackson: Power & Barksdale, 1880), 572.

8. *American State Papers, Public Lands*, Washington, 1834, p. 170.

9. "Dispatches of U.S. Consuls in New Orleans, 1798–1807," p. 2, New Orleans Public Library, microfilm T.225-1.

10. Jack D. L. Holmes, *Gayoso: The Life and Times of a Spanish Governor in the Mississippi Valley, 1789–1799* (Baton Rouge: Louisiana State University Press, 1965), 267.

11. Archivo General de Simancas, No. 3, illustrated in Samuel Wilson, Jr., "Architecture in Eighteenth-Century West Florida," in Samuel Proctor (ed.), *Eighteenth-Century Florida and Its Borderlands* (Gainesville: University Press of Florida, 1975), 138.

12. Deed Book A, fo. 546, September 12, 1797, Adams County Courthouse, Natchez, MS.

13. Silas Brown, February 16, 1808, No. 5, Manuscript Division, Library of Congress, Washington, D.C.

14. *Mississippi Herald and Natchez Gazette*, January 22, 1806, 3.

15. Deed Book F, fo. 42, Adams County Courthouse.

16. Probate Records of James Andrews, Adams County Courthouse.

17. Deed Book E, fo. 19, June 1, 1808, Adams County Courthouse.

18. Deed Book H, fo. 36, 37, February 6, 1815, Adams County Courthouse.

19. *Washington [Mississippi] Republican*, April 13, 1813, p. 1.

20. Fortescue Cummings, "Cummings' Tour to the West," in Reuben Gold Thwaites (ed.), *Early Western Travels, 1748–1846* (Cleveland: Arthur H. Clark, 1904), 4, p. 319.

21. Mary Wallace Crocker, *Historic Architecture in Mississippi* (Hattiesburg: University and College Press of Mississippi, 1973), 47.

22. Frederick Doveton Nichols, *The Early Architecture of Georgia* (Chapel Hill: University of North Carolina Press, 1957), 66, 79.

23. A copy of this letter, addressed to Ep Hoyt, Esq., is in the possession of Samuel Wilson, Jr.

24. *Natchez Mississippi Free Trader*, January 17, 1852, p. 2.

25. Probate Records of Levi Weeks, Adams County Courthouse.

26. *Natchez Mississippi Republican*, November 17, 1824, p. 4.

27. Illustrated in *Mississippi Panorama*, catalog from an exhibition at the City Art Museum of St. Louis, 1949, 120–21.

28. Samuel Wilson, Jr., "Clifton—An Ill-Fated Natchez Mansion," *Journal of Mississippi History* 46 (August, 1984), 179.

29. John Hebron Moore, *Andrew Brown and Cypress Lumbering in the Old Southwest* (Baton Rouge: Louisiana State University Press, 1967), 23; *Natchez Gazette*, June 28, 1827, pp. 2, 3.

Notes on Contributors

Letha Wood Audhuy, Maître de conférence at the University of Toulouse-le-Mirail, France, is a specialist in American history and culture. She has published essays on Henry James, John Steinbeck, T. S. Eliot, and F. Scott Fitzgerald.

Ian Brown is associate curator of the North American Collections at Harvard University's Peabody Museum. Dr. Brown has done extensive research on Mississippi Indians since 1971, when he first came to Natchez to assist in the survey and excavation of prehistoric sites in the Natchez Bluffs region. He has published numerous monographs on North American Indians, and has particular interests in the Indians of the lower Mississippi Valley.

Don E. Carleton is director of the Eugene C. Barker Texas History Collection at the University of Texas. He specializes in Texas and Southwest history. A popular lecturer, he has also written three books and numerous articles for such journals as *Southwestern Historical Quarterly* and *Discovery.*

Alfred E. Lemmon is reference archivist and director of Reader Services in the Manuscripts Division of the Historic New Orleans Collection. He has published more than fifty major articles on various aspects of Latin American history and culture, and has lectured widely in this country, in Europe, and in Latin America.

Jeanne Middleton Forsythe chairs the Department of Education at Millsaps College. A specialist in Mississippi education history and education policy, she has served three years with the Jackson, Mississippi, public schools' Office of Research and Evaluation. She participated in the 1983 NEA Conference on Human and Civil Rights in Education and was a contributing author to *Mississippi: Conflict and Change*.

The late **Milton B. Newton, Jr.** was head of Geoforensics in Baton Rouge. A cultural geographer, his special interests were in issues connected with the historical landscape. He authored numerous works, including *Cultural Preadaptation in the Upland South* and *Atlas of Louisiana*.

Estill Curtis Pennington is an art historian in New Orleans. Formerly director of the Lauren Rogers Museum in Laurel, Mississippi, he is a specialist in American art and American cultural history. He has served as art historian at the Smithsonian Institution's Archives of American Art. He is the author of *Mississippi Portraiture* and has published and lectured widely on and mounted numerous exhibits of southern and regional artists.

Morton Rothstein is editor of *Agricultural History* and professor of history at the University of California, Davis. He has published numerous essays on agricultural and economic history and has special expertise in the antebellum cotton economy.

Julie Sass is a graduate student in history at the University of Southern Mississippi.

Samuel Wilson, Jr., has practiced architecture since 1931, working principally on historic renovation and restoration projects in the New Orleans area. Recognized as one of the leading architectural historians in the United States, he has written many pamphlets and articles on Louisiana and Gulf Coast architecture, and is the author of numerous books, including *Bienville's New Orleans: A French Colonial Capital, 1718–1768* and *Plantation Houses on the Battlefield of New Orleans*.

Index

156

Index

Barclay, Salkeld & Co., 98
Barnes, Abram, 65, 66, 68, 69
Barnes, Ann, 69
Bartram, William, *Travels Through North and South Carolina*, 31
Baton Rouge, 63, 82, 86, 87, 111, 137
Basil G. Kiger Papers, 61
Battle of New Orleans, 67
Batz, Alexandre De, 9
Bayou Manchac ("River Iberville"), 75, 80, 82, 83, 84, 85, 87, 94
Beaumont, William H., 141
Bédier, J., 30
Bell, Thomas, 112
Benjamin L. C. Wailes Papers, 64, 65
Biblioteca Nacional, 46, 55
Bienville, Baptiste Le Moyne, Sieur de, 32, 33, 34, 136
Big Black River, 83
Biloxi, 32
Bingaman, Adam, 67, 68, 101
Bingaman, Catherine Surget, 101, 117, 118
Birds of America, 121
Blackman, Dr. H. G., 62
Boston, 30, 50, 71, 118
Bourbon County, Ky., 116
Bowie, Jim, 61
Bowie, John J., 61
Bowman, Shearer Davis, 69
Boyce, L. M., 62
Boyds (Coles) Creek, 82
Brain, Jeffrey P., 16
Brandon, Gerard, 67, 68
Briars, The (plantation), 70, 71, 151
British East Florida, 93, 94
British grants, 89
British Public Record Office, 82
British West Florida, 93, 94
Brown, Andrew, 101, 150
Brown, James N., 62
Brown, Silas, 141
Brown's Gardens, 150
Bruin, Peter Bryan, 99, 107
Buena Vista (plantation), 61
Buffalo Creek, 81, 82, 83, 85
Bullock, Henry, 133
Burling Hill (home), 144, 146
Burr, Aaron, 47
Business Collection, The, 62
Butler, Thomas, 100, 101
Byron, Lord, 112

Cabildo, Cathedral, and Presbytère (New Orleans), 139
Cadillac, Antoine de la Mothe, 33, 42
Cadiz, 46
Calhoun, John C., 70
Canada, 43, 63, 95
Canton, 63
Captaincy General of Havana, 49
Caribbean, 43, 94, 95, 97, 112
Carlisle, Pa., 98, 100, 101
Carlos IV, 138
Carney, Arthur, 62
Carolinas, 34
Carondelet, Baron de, 66
Cartographic Information Center (CIC), 80, 81, 84
Carver, Jonathan, *Travels to the Interior Parts of America*, 31
Casa de Contratacion, La (House of Trade), 48–49
Catholicism, 114, 127
Catholic school; *see*, Academy for Young Ladies
Catholic priests, 138
Cattle, 98
Ceremonial centers, 12, 15, 17
Chactas cycle (Chateaubriand), 36–37
Chamberlain, T. J., 62
Chamberlain-Hyland-Gould Family Papers, 61
Chambers, Moreau B., 12
Chambers, Dr. Rowland, 61
Charles III, 47
Charles V, 47
Charles Backus Dana Papers, 64
Charleston, 50
Charlevoix, Père de, 37, 40; *Histoire et description generale de la Nouvelle France*, 31
Chateaubriand, Francois-René de, 29, 30, 31, 32, 35, 36, 37, 38, 39, 40, 41; *Atala*, 29, 30, 31, 37, 38; *Le Genie du Christianisme*, 30; *Les Natchez*, 29–30, 31, 36, 37, 38, 41; *René*, 31, 37
Chépar, 39
Cherokee Indians, 8
Chickasaw Bluffs (Memphis), 44
Chickasaw Indians, 8, 24, 34, 36
Choate, Rufus, 71
Choctaw Indians, 8, 9, 34, 35, 37, 87
Chotard boys, 119
Christ Episcopal Church (Alexandria,

Index

Index

Index